W9-BFO-655

WHAT ARE WE HOPING FOR?

What Are We Hoping For?

Reflections on Lent and Easter

Richard Leonard, SJ

Paulist Press
New York / Mahwah, NJ

Library of Congress Control Number: 2015955512
ISBN 978-0-8091-4966-7 (paperback)
ISBN 978-1-58768-548-4 (e-book)

Published by Paulist Press
997 Macarthur Boulevard
Mahwah, New Jersey 07430
www.paulistpress.com

Printed and bound in the
United States of America

To Trish & Graeme, Mary, Emma & Humphrey,
Peter & Josephine, Lisa & Nick, Paul, Maryanne,
Angela Mary, Christina, Loyola, Trish & Bob, Kate,
Jim & Juanita, Jen, Paul & Carolyn, Kathryn,
Robert & Yvonne, Tony & Maryanne, Joyce & Bruce,
John, Rosalie & Don, Tammy & John,
Moira, Siobhan & Patrick.

All of you are signs of faith, hope, and love for me.

CONTENTS

PREFACE

A man was driving along the road when he saw the Easter Bunny hop into his lane. He swerved to avoid hitting the Bunny, but couldn't do so. The basket of eggs went everywhere. The driver felt guilty and began to cry. A woman saw the man and pulled over. "What's wrong?" she asked. "I accidentally killed the Easter Bunny," he explained. The woman knew exactly what to do. She went to her car, and pulled out a spray can, walked over to the Bunny, and sprayed the entire contents all over the little furry animal.

Miraculously the Easter Bunny came back to life, jumped up, picked up his eggs, waved at them, and hopped on down the road. Not far away the Bunny stopped, turned around, and waved again. He kept doing this for as far as they could see.

The man was astonished. "What in heaven's name is in that can you sprayed on the Easter Bunny?" The woman showed the man the label. It read, "Hare spray. Restores life to dead hare—adds permanent wave."

For many of our children, the Bunny and his eggs are the most important thing about Easter. In the history of Christianity, the Church has often domesticated local traditions and festivals, bringing them on board and making them her own. Although there are various theories about the origins of the name *Easter*, the most commonly held is one that comes from the Anglo-Saxon spring festival in honor of the goddess Eastre. Her symbol was the rabbit, a symbol of fertility and abundance, and the giving of eggs was a sign of new life bursting forth as winter withdrew. These associations only make sense in the Northern Hemisphere (while it heads into spring at Eastertime, those in the Southern Hemisphere move toward winter), but we can see why the early Christians could be so adaptable and inculturated with this local festival.

For some Christian families, and for the wider world, Lent is the season to buy Easter eggs and Easter Sunday is the day to consume them all. If so, we have some work to do to clarify what we are actually hoping for in this annual twelve-week journey.

This book continues from my reflections for Advent and Christmas in a book entitled *What Are We Waiting For?* and because of the generous response to that book, I offer these reflections for Lent and Easter. These seasons are two of the most important times in the liturgical year of the Church, but because of all the commercial focus we give to Christmas, some people lose sight of the fact that Easter Sunday is the most important day in the Christian calendar. As St. Paul reminds us, "If there is no resurrection of the dead, then Christ has not been raised; and if Christ has not been raised, then our proclamation has been in vain and your faith has been in vain" (1 Cor 15:13–14). So while many of us make significant personal and family preparations for the great feast of Christmas, it follows that, even more so, we should be preparing for the greatest of all feasts: Easter. The Church does so by giving us the Lenten season and, as we will see, it is not meant to be all doom and gloom.

These reflections do not follow the three-year cycle of Lenten and Easter readings in the lectionary. Rather they pick up the major themes of these ninety days as they emerge almost every year. I will also reflect on the Transfiguration, Palm Sunday, and the holiest of days, the Easter Triduum: Holy Thursday, Good Friday, and Easter Day. Even though the Easter season strictly concludes on Pentecost Sunday, I will reflect on that and the Feast of the Ascension; I will also look at a contemporary reading of The Body and Blood of Christ and The Most Holy Trinity. These latter two solemnities occur in Ordinary Time, but they come straight after the Easter Season and before our Sundays return to the ordinary rhythms of our lives.

May these reflections assist you year after year to recover the hope to which we are called in these days of formation, and this great time of jubilee.

ACKNOWLEDGMENTS

Mark-David Janus, CSP, Paul McMahon, and the team at Paulist Press for their continuing belief in me and my work, and for enabling me to talk to a very wide audience about faith and life;

Brian McCoy, SJ, and the Australian Province of the Society of Jesus for the education and formation I have received and their ongoing support to do the "greatest good for the greatest number";

Fr. Brian Lucas and the Australian Catholic Bishops Conference who understand that the communication's ministry involves various forms of the presentation of the word;

The forbearance of my Jesuit community at Lavender Bay, Sydney, whose support and care, at home and while away, provides a home base for a ministry often lived "with one foot in the air."

THE FORTY DAYS

A Pilgrimage of Hope

*T*he season of Lent is often described as a "pilgrimage of faith." Pilgrimages have always been alluring for Christian believers. Since Mary Magdalene went to and from the tomb on Easter Sunday, the followers of Jesus have hit the road to discover the divine. Jerusalem, Fatima, Lourdes, Czestochowa, Medugorje, and Assisi are just a few of the most famous places of pilgrimage, but the one that currently captures many people's imagination is the Camino de Santiago in Spain, where, since 1092, people have trod to venerate the memory and remains of St. James the Apostle. Footsore and exhausted by journey's end, some of these journeys are also life changing, or at least life affirming.

However, we don't actually need to leave home to be a pilgrim. Lent is an annual journey of a thousand small steps to new life at Easter. With Christ as our companion and guide, the whole church sets out on a pilgrimage from ashes to hope.

My most stark experience of being sent out as a pilgrim did not happen very far from home. In the mid-1980s, when I was in the Jesuit novitiate, the second year novices were dropped 125 miles (200km) from our first house in Australia at Sevenhill in the Clare Valley north of Adelaide, South Australia. Founded in 1850 by the Austrian Jesuits, to this day it is a parish, retreat house, and, thank God, a very fine winery!

The second years were given enough money for one emergency phone call and a letter from the novice master for the police explaining who we are and what we were doing. We were, officially, vagrants. With a backpack and a sleeping bag, we had to walk the entire way, begging for our food and accommodation each day. In the pursuit of board and lodging, we could not tell anyone who we were or what we were doing. We could not trade off being a Jesuit. The novice master told us, for example, that if we were invited into someone's home, then only after we had established the extent of their hospitality could we tell them who we were so that they would not be frightened that they had welcomed Jack the Ripper to stay the night. However, if the homeowner offered the garage and a sandwich and then later, finding out that we were Jesuits, wanted to offer the guest suite and a meal at the dining room table, we were to refuse. We were told that we could not get an upgrade from economy to first class!

Those ten days were the only time in my life I've known hunger. During winter, would you let me into your house, let me sleep in your garage, or give me some food? I stayed in hostels for homeless men run by the St. Vincent

De Paul Society, broke into broken-down schoolhouses, camped out in bandstands, and slept out under the stars.

On day six, I arrived at a small country town at 7:00 p.m. in the teeming rain. I was soaked to the skin. I was drawn by the bright fluorescent cross that hung over what I was soon to discover was the Catholic Church. There was nothing in the rules to say you could not beg from churches. I walked up the presbytery steps and introduced myself to the parish priest. After giving out my spiel, I asked, "Father, I am wondering if you could put me in contact with the local SVDP?" In his wonderful Irish brogue, he replied, "You're looking at the local Vincent de Paul." So Father gave me five dollars for dinner and five dollars for breakfast, a towel for a shower, and a bed in the now unused old school room. Because he never let me into the house, I went on my way the next day without telling him who I was and what I was doing.

On the third to last day of the pilgrimage, as it is actually called, I approached the largest house in the small town of Riverton. There I met Mrs. Mary Byrne, who proceeded to grill me about where I had come from, why I was in such need, and where I was going. I never told a lie, but I was Jesuitical with the truth. After the interrogation, she declared, "I think I can trust ya," and ushered me into her home. She told me I could stay in the guest room, have dinner that night and breakfast in the morning, and then be on my way. I then told Mary who I was and what I was doing to which she said, "Get outta here!" For a moment, I thought she meant I had to actually get out of there. But Mary quickly went on, "The Jesuits look after the church here from Sevenhill." And then she changed, "You haven't been sent out as a spy have you?" "No," I said, "Why would you think I've been sent out as a spy?" "Well, you Jesuits are always going on caring for the poor and a faith that does justice in the world, and I thought you lot may have been sent out to spy on us to test whether we have been listening to all those social justice sermons all these years." I assured her that I hadn't.

I had a great night with all Mary's family, and the next day I was on my way. When I got to the next small hamlet of Watervale in the late Sunday afternoon, I discovered that everyone was off watching or playing the local football competition. The only person I could see was a woman weeding her front garden on the rise of the hill on the edge of the town. I walked up the hill, through her gate, and gave my spiel: "Hello, I'm Richard Leonard and I am on my way to the Clare Valley to get some work on one of the wineries to get my passage back to Sydney. I have nowhere to stay and nothing to eat, and I am wondering if you can help me with either or both."

At the end of my speech, the woman looked up from her garden and said, "Are you the Jesuit who stayed with Mary Byrne last night? Her daughter is engaged to my son, and I play the organ at Sevenhill Church." And that night the Byrne family came down and joined me and the Briskys for another wonderful dinner in the Riesling Valley of Australia. Being on pilgrimage was looking good.

When I reached Sevenhill, I wrote to that generous pastor telling him that he did not know it, but he had been kind to a Jesuit novice. A short while later, a note arrived from the good pastor that read, "The Jesuits taught me at school in Ireland. I hated every single minute of it. If I'd known who you were and what you were up to, I would have kicked your backside and told you to get yourself out of town. Even now, the crafty Jesuits have got one over on me. I knew, however, that there was something a little bit different about you, because, let's face it, you were, without question, the most articulate beggar I've ever met in my life."

On that road to Sevenhill, I learned more about the Lenten journey than at any other time in my life. I discovered that living simply, penance, and fasting (even if I had no option), being totally dependent on God's goodness through the undeserved kindness of strangers, and being on pilgrimage in the real world helped me feel close to God in a way I had never known before. I prayed for my daily bread, for somewhere to lay my head, and I was often overwhelmed with gratitude for the smallest kindnesses. While it was a stark context, that pilgrimage showed me that the clutter in my head, heart, and life often gets in the way of me finding God and allowing God to find me.

Even if we do not leave home every Lent, we do become pilgrims with Christ, and to Christ—decluttering as we go through our prayer, penance, fasting, and acts of charity. No matter how soul-sore we may be by journey's end, may this pilgrimage of hope be both life changing and life affirming, because that's the reward for the pilgrim's progress at Easter.

Rising from Ashes

I have always liked the poetry of Tom Conry's strong contemporary Lenten anthem, "We Rise Again from Ashes":

We offer you our failures,
we offer you attempts,
the gifts not fully given,
the dreams not fully dreamt.
Give our stumblings direction,
give our visions wider view,
an offering of ashes, an offering to you.[1]

Ashes are a powerful, sobering, and mortal symbol: "...ashes to ashes, dust to dust...." We start our Lenten journey by being confronted by our death. "Remember you are dust, and unto dust you shall return." It is a great way to be reminded that we shouldn't sweat the small stuff!

There is something elemental about ash. However, until quite recently, Catholics were in two minds about death, fire, and ashes. At least we didn't go in for cremation. In some countries it was forbidden by the local bishops. These days, most Catholics can choose between being buried or cremated. Given the importance of Ash Wednesday in the Christian calendar, the Catholic ban on cremation is hard to understand. As powerful as it is to see a casket committed to the ground, sprinkling someone's ashes over a place that was important to the deceased, or interring them in a church's columbarium, can be even more moving.

Ashes amplify two important facets about Lent. On one level, ashes remind us of our relationship to the earth: human beings are made up of the same substance as the ground upon which we walk. We might be the crown of creation, but we are utterly related to it, part of a continuous whole. Our human nature may be the most sophisticated arrangement of the nature's building blocks, but that should not lead us to believe or act as though we are the glory of creation, different from it, or masters of it. In *Laudato Si'*, Pope Francis strongly counters this understanding:

> If we approach nature and the environment without this openness to awe and wonder, if we no longer speak the language of fraternity and beauty in our relationship with the world, our attitude will be that of masters, consumers, ruthless exploiters, unable to set limits on their immediate needs. By contrast, if we feel intimately united with all that exists, then sobriety and care will well up spontaneously. The poverty and austerity of Saint Francis were no mere veneer of asceticism, but something much more radical: a refusal to turn reality into an object simply to be used and controlled (#11).[2]

"Remember you are dust, and unto dust you shall return."

On another level, as we have noted, ashes remind us of our death. In our contemporary society, this element of Lent is confronting. We live in a death-denying culture. We tend to hide the dead, or when we have to see them, we dress them up to make them look as though they are still alive, just asleep. At the most extreme, the plastic surgery and cosmetic industries are about Western society's resistance to growing old, confronting the decline of our bodies and our death.

However, Ash Wednesday brings us face-to-face with our mortality. We are invited to think about what changes in our lives we would effect if our deaths were imminent. Sometimes in casual conversation about this topic, we hear people talk about overseas trips and fancy meals, but if most of us had just twenty-four hours to live, chances are we would primarily attend to our relationships. My hunch is that many of us would want to tell the people that we love that we love them, forgive those we need to, and ask forgiveness from those we have hurt or offended. And then many of us would think about our relationship with God.

These forty days give us pause to assess whether the life we are living—our relationships—are generally in concert with Christ's way, truth, and life. Lent challenges us to assess compassionately whether who we are is who we want to be, and who God knows we can yet become. If our death were to come soon, would we move gently into eternal life? Even thinking about our death can be bleak and leave us in despair. That's why another major theme in Lent is how Christ came into our world to rescue us from sin and death, from hopelessness and despair, and the worst things in our nature.

In our overly independent world where the self-made man or woman makes such a claim on our imagination, the idea that we all need rescuing is strongly resisted; the best of us needs no one! However, that's a myth. We rightly make heroes out of people who rescue others. Think for a moment of all the television shows—real life or drama—that have "rescue" as their theme—all those police, fire, medical, and emergency shows. But then, that's someone else who needs the rescuing. Not us.

While some people seem to need rescuing all the time, others certainly need it some of the time. That's the human condition. Christian faith holds that God saw that when we were stuck, trapped in our sin and destructive behavior, then the Trinity risked everything and became one of us in Jesus the Lord so that we would be rescued from the violence and death that can mark humanity's existence.

For believers, it doesn't matter if we get into trouble once or seventy times, Christ is there to get us out of the toughest spot, and to save us from ourselves. No doubt God would prefer that we learned from our mistakes and listen to all the advisories he has given us, including the example of his own Son, but even so, he comes when we call, often in ways we do not immediately notice.

That's why Lent is a life-giving season. It brings us back to the basics. In asking us to confront the implications of our death, it invites us to recognize the places where we're stuck or trapped, caught or cornered, and celebrate that Christ has come to rescue us, to set us free. In doing so, we find that where we thought there could only be death and destruction—there is in fact life, and life eternal.

Thanks be to the Father,
who made us like himself.
Thanks be to his Son,
who saved us by his death.

Thanks be to the Spirit
who creates the world anew
from an offering of ashes, an offering to you.

A Season of Joy

It surprises some people when they hear some of the liturgical prayers during Lent describe this holy time as a "season of joy." As a child, the last association I would have ever made with Lent was feeling joyful. I thought it was meant to be forty days of doom and gloom. I have now come to see I was wrong on both counts: Lent is meant to be a consoling and joyful time, and it is not actually forty days long.

If you count the days from Ash Wednesday to the Easter Triduum (which begins on Holy Thursday), there are forty-five days in the Lenten season, not forty. That's because, since the first Easter Sunday, every Sunday is a day of the resurrection, even during Lent. Strictly speaking, Sundays are never meant to be days of fast and penance, so we could eat chocolate on Sundays during Lent. That was one thing I was never told as a kid!

Numbers are never randomly used in the Bible. One, three, seven, twelve, forty, and fifty all have specific meanings. The number forty indicates a time of formation. In the Bible, we have forty days of rain for Noah's flood, for Moses' fast, for Jonah inside the whale, and for the period between the resurrection and the ascension in Luke–Acts. The Israelites wander in the desert for forty years. Jesus, of course, enters the desert for forty days, which is the direct reference point for our Lenten journey. Mark, Matthew, and Luke may be literally correct in writing that Jesus went into the wilderness for forty days. Matthew and Luke go further and note that Jesus fasted for this period as well. If they also mean that he went without water, then, given that we know that human beings die without water between eight and ten days, we have a problem with Jesus being a true and full human being. And though we have verifiable cases of people surviving with water but without food for thirty to forty days, the physical deficits in almost every case are profound. It might be a better reading of the wilderness texts to suggest that the evangelists knew that forty was not meant to be literally but symbolically correct: that the time in the desert, both for Jesus and for us in Lent, is a profound period of formation and preparation.

The problem these days is that Lent for some people has become part of an annual keep-fit or get-fit program. While good things in themselves, they are not Lenten. We don't give up food and forgo alcohol or chocolate to get slim or to prove to ourselves that we are not alcoholics or have great willpower. We give up or take on things in Lent because it helps us to confront the elements in our lives or in ourselves that hold us back from following Christ and being the most faithful, hopeful, and loving person possible.

Our Lenten sacrifices remind us that, as our bodies crave certain food or drink, in the same way our spirit or soul craves God. And unlike the obsessive way we can act when we are looking to satisfy our cravings or appetites from the things around us, our spiritual cravings or appetites, as single-minded as they can sometimes be, are supposed to be marked by a lighter and more joyful quest. Lent is about liberation, about staring down those things that stop us from being free to follow Christ. The process may be painful but the end point is life—and more life still.

To do this, we have to unhook joyfulness from happiness. It worries me that I often hear Catholic and Christian parents say, "All I want is for my children to be happy." The same line is often used by priests and religious about their own vocations: "I just want to be happy in the service." While I like people to be generally happy, it is just not realistic or desirable for happiness to become the defining feature of our lives. Happiness is now an industry.

The social researcher Hugh Mackay sums up our contemporary problem with happiness being the essential human goal:

> Weekends should be great....Holidays should be havens of happiness....Work should be fun, or, if not fun, then at least stimulating and satisfying. So should marriage, and if it isn't, then we should strive for a perfect divorce in which we and our former partner will behave in the civilized and responsible way we couldn't quite manage during the marriage....The kids themselves should be gifted in ways that make them worthy of special attention....Our counsellors, it goes without saying, should be gurus....Sex should be blissful and deeply satisfying, every time....Sport? It's all about winning, of course.

...Our cars should be perfectly safe....The state should leave us alone to get on with our lives in peace but should exert tight control over the behavior of other people who mightn't be as responsible or competent as we are....In our perfect world, blame is easy to affix, revenge is sweet, and outcomes are always positive (for us). Life should proceed from one thrilling gratification to the next, banners triumphantly aflutter, joy unbounded. All we want is heaven on earth. Is that too much to ask?[3]

Lent is a spoiler for the happiness industry. It proclaims that, rather than being happy, we will know true joy only if we undergo the pain of dealing with our inordinate attachments, blinds spots, biases, prejudices, ignorance, unexamined presuppositions, and the destructive behaviors that flow from them. Pope Francis helps define the joy we seek in each and every Lent: "The Christian message is called the 'Gospel,' that is, 'the good news,' an announcement of joy for all people; the Church is not a refuge for sad people, the Church is a house of joy."[4] On another occasion the Holy Father said, "If we keep this joy to ourselves it will make us sick in the end, our hearts will grow old and wrinkled and our faces will no longer transmit that great joy—only nostalgia and melancholy, which is not healthy....These melancholic Christians' faces have more in common with pickled peppers than the joy of having a beautiful life."[5]

It would be great one day to hear a Catholic or Christian parent say that what they want for their children is not just to be happy but to be "the most hopeful and loving person possible, full of integrity and living a faith that does justice." These goals will not assure anyone of happiness, but they will bring great joy, in the same way that Lent does: no passing pain—no ultimate gain, but living a beautiful life.

The forty days of Lent are an annual time of formation where, like Jesus, and with him, we enter our symbolic desert so that we can be even more liberated by God's saving love. If that doesn't bring a spring to our step, I don't know what will.

Into the Wilderness

Many of us have a couple of books that have made an impact on our lives. One of them for me is *Poverty of Spirit* by Johannes B. Metz. First published in 1968, it is short, accessible, and profound. In a series of meditations on the temptations of Jesus in the wilderness, Metz argues that it is this chapter in Jesus' life where he wrestles with his humanity. "We can say that the three temptations in the desert are three assaults on the poverty of Jesus, on the self-renunciation through which he chose to redeem us. They represent an assault on the radical and uncompromising step he has taken: to come down from God and become man."[6]

Metz sees the first temptation as Jesus embracing the mortality of our human nature and the poverty of the commonplace. The second is about accepting powerlessness and being needy. The third is a rejection of false pride and glory, of being superior. In doing so, Jesus does not spare himself anything in entering into solidarity with us. "Jesus subjected himself to our plight and opted for us as we are...He did not simply dip into our existence, wave the magic wand of divine life over us, and then retreat hurriedly to his eternal home....He immersed himself in our misery and followed man's road to the end."[7]

Christianity is the only world religion to believe that God took human flesh and became one with us—one of us. By sharing completely in our lot, in our poverty, Jesus shows us that the acceptance of our own humanity, our poverty of spirit, is the point where God's grace can work in us, where we see the way out of being entrapped by the worst of our human nature, "for whenever I am weak, then I am strong" (2 Cor 12:10).

This Lent, when we enter our figurative deserts, when we are faced with difficult choices and temptations, there are four things we need to remember:

First, temptation is not sin. Even though our thoughts may sometimes be cruel or murderous, there is a grave difference between being tempted to do something and doing it. Only when we freely and knowingly choose to act on serious temptation is serious sin involved. Though we may like to talk about the temptations we have in the sacrament of penance, we never have to "confess" them as though they are the same as sinful actions.

Second, temptations can often appear as good things, but they always have a destructive sting in the tail. It's good to be alert to all the consequences of what we do and say, and learn from our experiences. The more we give into temptation, the more immune we become to seeing that there's anything wrong with what we are doing.

We can develop whole habits in our living—deceiving ourselves that what we are doing "isn't that bad. It's not hurting anyone." But it is—it's hurting me, stopping me from being the best person I can be. Usually, our temptations have a context and a history. They can come when we are feeling most vulnerable, and they normally strike at the most susceptible points in our character. It helps if we are aware of the danger signs in our lives which can weaken our defenses. Tiredness, boredom, anger, alcohol and drug use, lack of good communication, and a poor self-esteem are common realities that can leave us more exposed than usual.

A daily examen is not supposed to be the moment when we beat ourselves up for where we went wrong today. It is the process by which, over time, we start to see the patterns in our behavior and choices: what leads us to God, life, and love; and what leads us to destruction, death, and despair. There is always a pattern in both movements.

Third, as many of the great Christian mystics testify, among the worst temptations are honor, riches, and pride. These writers remind us that we should be wise in how we deal with temptations: name what's going on, and attend to destructive behavior quickly and consistently. To balance honor, we need people in our lives who will tell us the truth in charity, especially the things we may not want to hear. To keep riches in check, we need to make sure that we use and possess money, and that our riches do not possess us. To avoid giving into false pride, we might ask if there are occasions when we can appropriately own when we are wrong and can back down and say we're sorry.

Finally, as we progress in the Christian life, we should not get discouraged if we feel we are failing and are more tempted to make destructive decisions. If Jesus was tempted where he was most vulnerable, so will we be. Furthermore, if a room is poorly lit, we don't see much dirt and dust. However, if the room is floodlit, everything is so much clearer to the naked eye. The room's sins and secrets are exposed. So it is with the spiritual life. Our growing sense of temptation and sin can be a sign that we are coming closer to the Light of the World. The worst thing we can do is to give into the temptation and then turn down the dimmer.

The great comfort for us in Jesus being tempted in the wilderness is that there is no path of temptation along which Jesus has not gone ahead of us to show us we can choose life ahead of death. God's self-surrender of divinity in and through the full and true humanity of Jesus shows us that the glory of God is humanity fully alive.

Welcome to Lent—a yearly season to keep embracing the poverty of our common neediness, powerlessness, and of our desire to be superior, so that, even when we are at our lowest ebb, God's grace can abound even more (cf. Rom 5:20).

Returning to the Beginning

Have you ever noticed that Jesus begins and ends his public ministry in a deserted place? The former is in an actual desert where he is tempted by Satan. The latter is at Golgotha, the "place of the skull"—in Latin it was called *Calvaria*, which means "a bare skull." It was located outside the second wall in Jerusalem and may have been littered with the skulls of the Romans' victims of capital punishment.

Deserted places are the geographical bookends of Jesus public life. But the parallels don't stop there. In both experiences, Jesus is tempted. In the Gospel of Mark, we are never told what Satan's temptations in the desert are about. Luke and Matthew fill in those details. On the cross, however, the crowd tempts Jesus to work a miracle, to come down from the cross and save himself.

In the first desert, Jesus is alone for the duration and then is ministered to by the angels at the end. At the place of the skull, Jesus is ministered to by his women disciples, who are the first to arrive and the last to leave. When he emerges out of the desert, Jesus proclaims that the kingdom of God is close at hand. At Calvary, he is put to death as a result of the kingdom he proclaimed and lived.

It is clear from all the Gospels that lonely places stayed with Jesus throughout his life. He withdraws from public ministry several times, sometimes alone, sometimes with others. He goes to the wilderness when he needs to be safe from the danger of an attack from the Sadducees after they accuse him of blasphemy. He withdraws to Caesarea Philippi where Peter and the disciples start to see who he is and the cost of following him. He ascends Mount Tabor, where at the transfiguration, his glory as the beloved Son of God is revealed. And on a few occasions he withdraws to pray, with or without his disciples, away from the great demands of the crowd. So these experiences—including the first and last deserted place—can be summarized as times of formation, safety, insight, revelation, sanity, and fidelity. That list is not a bad summary of what Lent can be for us too.

One of the ways to understand the Lenten journey is to imagine it as a yearly retreat in daily life, where we spiritually and emotionally, and maybe at times also physically, come away to a safe place for the sanity of a formation that enables us to have greater insight, to touch again the revelation of God's love and mercy, which enables us to remerge with greater fidelity to Christ, who remains utterly faithful to us.

This notion of an annual retreat is more important than ever before. We also know that work is now identified as the most praised of all the addictions. But people who are at work all day, most of the night, and every weekend may not be hard workers. As good as that may be, they may not want to confront who they are and what's going on at home. Work becomes their excuse and refuge.

Of course, we have been sold a lie. We've been told for decades that the more technology we have, the more leisure we would enjoy. Wrong! We have never had more technology, and yet people complain more than ever before about "time poor."

I've been with many people on their deathbeds. One comment that I have never heard at that moment is, "Father, I wished I had spent more time at work." Not once!

Excessive demands on one's time, no matter how great the needs and rewards, were issues for Jesus as well. Jesus shows us that, when we appropriately retreat from our work, it can give us the distance to make sense of what we do, and see our work as means to an end, not an end in itself. Jesus even shows us that the needs of the crowd in the Gospels are not the only ones that had to be met. Lent helps us to reset appropriate boundaries.

Most of us do not need to go out and find a physical wilderness to know its claim on our lives. Wildernesses know no geographical limitations. They can take up residence in our imagination. While they can be places of loss and ruin from where some great heroes have never returned—like Magellan, Captain James Cook, David Livingstone, Robert Scott, Ernest Shackleton, and Amelia Earhart—Christ shows us by his own example that, though the retreat is filled with a mixture of pleasure and pain, these forty days can be abundant with revelation, transformation, and recreation.

LENTEN DISCIPLINE

Prayer: Touching Eternity

A few years ago, I was very brave in writing a book on prayer. My prayer life does not give me bragging rights; I am no mystic. I share with many other Christians the usual desolations, lack of discipline and focus, that makes me see my own prayer life as a very humble offering to God each day. *Why Bother Praying?* is more about the context within which we pray, and how rich, and often untapped, our Christian tradition is in regard to the ways and means of listening to and communicating with God.

However, apart from my family, the most important instruction about how to pray came from my first grade teacher, Sister Mary Consuelo. Behind her back, we called her Sister Mary-consume-a-whalelo. She was a Sister of Mercy. She was firm and fair. She needed to be. She once told me that in the forty-four years of her teaching career, she never had less than forty children in the class. She once had sixty-one children in the same room. There were forty-two children in my first grade class in 1969. Could you imagine that ratio now? I also thought Sister was tall. She was five foot one. In second grade, Sister also prepared us for our first confession, as it was called then, and our first holy communion. I remember being terrified going into the dark box to make my first confession; when the slide pulled back, I could barely see through the grill, so in my anxiety I started yelling at the top of my lungs, "Bless me Father for I have sinned; this is my first confession and these are my sins." At that point the dean of the cathedral said, "God's not deaf and neither am I!"

I wish I could say that I was really looking forward to my first holy communion because I wanted to receive the Lord in a special and unique way. But that would be a lie. Actually, I was terrified of doing something wrong at the Mass and of biting the host. At the age of seven, what I was really looking forward to was the party that followed the Mass and the presents I would get. Back at school the following day, Sr. Mary Consuelo asked me what gift I enjoyed the most. Of all the Bibles, holy pictures, rosaries, and medals I received, the gift I treasured was a bone china holy water font of the Madonna and Child. "I would like to see that," Sr. Mary Consuelo said. "Would you bring it to school tomorrow?"

The next day, during the first break—little lunch we used to call it—Sister was on playground duty. She was wearing a large blue and white-striped apron over her habit. Imagine this scene. There were over seven hundred children in my Catholic primary school, and there was only one teacher supervising all of us—a ratio of 1:700. That would be illegal today. Not that Sister Mary-consume-a-whalelo had any trouble controlling the masses. She was a formidable figure, who was as wide as she was tall, and ruled the playground with a whistle. Do you remember wondering how big the nun's pockets were in those habits? Seemingly, the nuns carried everything in them, and they could put their hands on what they needed at a moment's notice. I raced up to Sister who was surrounded by children: "I've brought the holy water font, Sister." "Very good, go and get it." All wrapped up in tissue paper, I carefully took the font out of my bag and then ran down to the bitumen playground. I was so excited at showing off my favorite present that I tripped and down I went right in front of Sister. The font hit the bitumen. It did not break. No, it smashed into tiny pieces. Sister swung into action. She was an old hand at health and safety, long before the term was invented. Into her pocket she went. Out came the whistle and with a full, shrill blast seven hundred children froze on their spot. Sister said to the children in our vicinity, "Whoever picks up the most pieces of china will get a holy picture." We thought that was something back then.

The second whistle rang out, and while six hundred and fifty children resumed their games, fifty children did a forensic search of the area, picking up every piece the naked eye could see and dropping them in the hammock that Sister had made from her apron with her left arm. Meanwhile, I was so distraught that Consuelo's right arm brought me in for a very big hug. Sister had many gifts, but among them was a very ample bosom. In fact, whenever we read about God's deep and consoling breasts in Isaiah 66:11, I go back to grade one. I am fairly certain I made my decision to become a celibate priest at that moment, between Sister's breasts. I was not sure I was ever going to get out of there alive!

The bell went and Sister rolled up the apron and walked me back to class. Three weeks later she told me to stay in at little lunch. I thought I was in trouble. When every other child had left the room, she opened the drawer of her desk and there, wrapped up in new tissue paper, was a fully restored holy water font. By then, I think I had forgotten about it.

In those days, we knew nothing much about the sisters. They went to Mass, said their prayers, and taught school. Before Sister Mary Consuelo became a nun, however, Helen Leane had done a degree in fine art, majoring in water colors and ceramics. She had taken those hundreds of fragments and spent hours and hours piecing my holy water font back together. When it was set, she repainted the entire object. The only sign that it had ever been broken was the rough plaster of paris on the back. She could have thrown those pieces away, and I would have gotten over it. In fact, I had. However, such was the effect of her prayer life on her relationships, even with a seven-year-old boy; she spent what must have been most of her leisure time for weeks reconstructing a treasured gift. But she was the real gift that day, and it was the best lesson I had from her.

Not being an overly sentimental person when it comes to things, and having been privileged to have studied or worked in Australia, the United Kingdom, Italy, and the United States, nevertheless, everywhere I go to live, that font goes too. Soon after being ordained a priest in December 1993, I was honored to be asked to preside at the Eucharist at Emmaus, the Sisters of Mercy nursing home in Brisbane. Sitting in her usual spot in the front row was Sister Mary Consuelo, now aged ninety. As part of my homily, I told the other hundred sisters the story of the holy water font. When I was done and sat down, Sister got up from her place and turned around to the others and said, "I told you I was good!" She was very good indeed.

Over the next few years, I visited Sister whenever I could. My last visit with her was in early March 1996. At that time she knew she was dying. She talked about it openly and calmly. I asked her if she was frightened to die. "Oh no," she quickly retorted, "I'm frightened of pain, but I am not fearful of death because through it I will go home and meet Christ face-to-face, and hopefully he will say to me, 'Well done good and faithful servant—with what you had you did your best.'" As I drove away from her that final day, there was Helen in my rear vision mirror, now a frail, wizened figure waving goodbye. I had tears streaming down my face in gratitude for a teacher who never stopped teaching, an adult who simply and appropriately loved kids who were not her own, and a believer who showed me that faith is about living this life so fully that we can even come to see death as an opportunity to hear Christ say, "With what you had you did your best."

That's why we pray in Lent—we take extra time to communicate with the One who loves us more than we could ever ask and imagine, so that we might keep a perspective on our hopes, griefs, anxieties, and even our sins. And, in the face of being overwhelmed by life, we hear a merciful and gentle voice remind us that what simply matters is that we do our best with what we've got. When we pray like this, we begin an eternal conversation now, so we will not be so frightened of the final word later.

Heart Speaks to Heart

Almost always, large-scale public devotions in the Church arise to counter a theological position that had gone astray. The devotional life of the Church reveals as much about us as it does about God. In Europe during the sixteenth and seventeenth centuries, and especially in France, the Jansenist heresy took hold. Among other things, Jansenism placed great emphasis on individual responsibility for sin, and the difficulty of obtaining Christ's mercy, whose true humanity was played down. The bottom line for Jansenists was that because we were so sinful, it was very hard to be saved.

By 1673, an obscure French nun, later known as St. Margaret Mary Alacoque, had several religious experiences that revealed the wounded, suffering heart of Jesus expressing his love, intimacy, and forgiveness for humanity. It was a direct rebuttal of the severity of Jansenism. That the devotion to the Sacred Heart spread like wildfire in the latter part of the seventeenth century indicates something of the necessity this revelation was for the Church. The *sensus fidei* had won again.

St. Margaret Mary may be credited with popularizing devotion to the Sacred Heart, but the tradition certainly predates her. It's described as early as the eleventh century and recorded in the visions and writings of many saints thereafter—Gertrude, Mechtilde, Frances de Sales, Francis Borgia, and John Eudes among them.

My most affectionate and early memory of the devotion to the merciful heart of Christ was from the time I was eight and spent many holidays at my Uncle Maurice and Aunty Claire's ranch in the outback of Australia. I come from a large extended Irish/Australian Catholic family. Maurice Leonard was the patriarch of the nine Leonard children. He used to call up each family before the school holidays and invite his nieces and nephews for the vacation. There could be up to ten cousins on holiday there at any one time.

Uncle Maurice and Aunty Claire were married in 1948. Every day until Uncle Maurice died a few years ago, they said the rosary. And even though the nightly devotion was falling off in our homes as children in the 1970s, when we went to their ranch for holidays we would all kneel after dinner and recite the five decades.

One of the features of Uncle Maurice's rosary was what he called the "toppings and tailings"—all the prayers before and after the rosary. It felt like they went longer than the rosary did. We recited the Apostles' Creed, the Benedictus, and the Magnificat before, and then prayers to the Sacred Heart, for the conversion of Russia (that worked!) and for the protection of the pope (that worked too!).

Eighteen years after I started holidaying on the family ranch, I decided to enter the Jesuits. One of my other cousins, Paul Leonard, who went to that ranch as often as I did, took me out to dinner. Given what I was doing with my life, matters religious were on the agenda. Out of nowhere, Paul asked across the table, "Do you remember that weird prayer Uncle Maurice used to say in the tailings when he hit his chest?" "What was weird about it?" I asked. "Well, it's a bit strange, don't you think, to hit your chest and call out, 'Say G'day to Jesus' and then everyone replies, 'Have Mercy on us.'" Now, this is an Australian moment, but my uncle had a very broad Australian accent. What my cousin thought was "Say G'day to Jesus" was in fact "Sacred Heart of Jesus." And at that moment, I could hear my uncle saying it, and could well understand how a young boy thought his uncle was "Saying G'day to Jesus," to which we all called back, "Have mercy on us." This was a tough religion!

Paul would not believe me when I explained that our Uncle Maurice was actually saying "Sacred Heart of Jesus, have mercy on us" so we went home and rang him. This was long before cell phones. Maurice told me that he and Claire had "just offered a decade of the rosary for your intentions as you join the Jesuits, Rich." I thanked him, and said Paul and I were just recalling the prayer to the Sacred Heart. "We've just done that too," he said. "Maurice, Paul thinks you were saying something else, when you led that prayer," I said. "What did you think I was saying, Paul?" "Weren't you 'Sayin' G'day to Jesus,' Uncle Maurice?" To put our Uncle's response in context, you have to know that he and Paul were more like father and son, but there was a wonderful pause at that moment, and then Uncle Maurice affectionately said, "Holy hell, Paul, you've always been an idiot." Ever since that night I have always preferred Paul's masterful version of that prayer, filled with humanity, familiarity, and love!

Our prayer in Lent is meant to take our eyes off the sinner in us and look to the Savior. There is nothing we have ever done, nothing we are doing or will do in the future that will stop Christ loving us.

Lenten prayer, in this season of joy, is the time where we can recall Jesus' suffering and death as an expression of his *solidarity with* us, and his *love for* us. The Eucharist is the most intimate of moments where Christ is broken and poured out in love so that we reproduce this pattern of sacrificial love in our own lives. God incomprehensibly and jealously regards us as his own, and so the best response we can offer is to live worthy of this unearned and underserved gift. We are challenged to be as generous, faithful, and sacrificial in our loving as Christ is toward us.

Thomas Merton expressed this better than anyone else in his book, *Love and Living*:

> Love is our true destiny. We do not find meaning of life by ourselves alone—we find it with one another. We do not discover the secret of our lives merely by study and calculation in our own isolated meditations. The meaning of our life is a secret that has to be revealed to us in love, by the one we love. And if this love is unreal, the secret will never be found....We will never be fully real until we let ourselves fall in love—either with another human person or with God.[8]

Is it any wonder then that Psalm 51:10 is one of the recurring themes throughout Lent? "Create in me a clean heart, O God, and put a new and right spirit within me."

As we prepare for Easter, may our prayer enable our hearts to overflow with redeemed humanity, natural familiarity, and merciful love.

Penance: Encounter Not Performance

Some people think Christianity invented prayer, penance, and fasting. We didn't. We may have perfected it, and we certainly made it our own, but these features have been part of worshiper's lives since the Zoratastrians. Pre-Christians prayed, fasted, and did penance to get God on their side. The more they did, the more they thought God would see how serious they were and would be kind to them. They thought that in undertaking these things they changed God: they got God to love them more.

However we Christians do not undertake any of these activities because they change God. All the sacrifices and prayers in the world cannot change God because we believe God is unchanging. This is a rock-solid part of classical theology: God is immutable. The Apostle James says, "Every generous act of giving, with every perfect gift, is from above, coming down from the Father of lights, with whom there is no variation or shadow due to change" (Jas 1:17). We cannot get God to love us more.

We pray, do penance, and fast so that our holy, loving, and unchanging God changes us, and thereby changes the world for the better. These ancient practices have stood the test of time in breaking down our resistances, and in being a response to God's invitation to a new and better life.

Penance needs careful attention. A confessor cannot

ask us to undertake an unjust or impossible penance, and we should never undertake serious, arduous, or long-term penances without the permission of our spiritual director, confessor, or pastor. Some of the greatest mystics in our tradition found that the bad spirit can take a good desire to make up for what we have done wrong, and can soon distort it into debasement. We need to make sure the intention and the outcome of our penances comes from a very healthy place within us for a wholly good purpose. Any act of reparation that is about self-destruction is not of God.

Doing penance flies in the face of those who think that all guilt is unhealthy and so making up for it in small or large measure is dangerous. However, there is such a thing as healthy guilt, a correct taking of responsibility for what I have done and what I have failed to do. This is neatly and sanely summed up in the fourth to ninth steps of Alcoholics Anonymous:

1. We admitted we were powerless over alcohol—that our lives had become unmanageable.
2. Came to believe that a Power greater than ourselves could restore us to sanity.
3. Made a decision to turn our will and our lives over to the care of God as we understood Him.
4. **Made a searching and fearless moral inventory of ourselves.**
5. **Admitted to God, to ourselves and to another human being the exact nature of our wrongs.**
6. **Were entirely ready to have God remove all these defects of character.**
7. **Humbly asked Him to remove our shortcomings.**

Continued

> 8. Made a list of all persons we had harmed, and became willing to make amends to them all.
> 9. Made direct amends to such people wherever possible, except when to do so would injure them or others.
> 10. Continued to take personal inventory and when we were wrong promptly admitted it.
> 11. Sought through prayer and meditation to improve our conscious contact with God as we understood Him, praying only for knowledge of His will for us and the power to carry that out.
> 12. Having had a spiritual awakening as the result of these steps, we tried to carry this message to alcoholics and to practice these principles in all our affairs.

Moving from personal sin to social sin, healthy guilt occurs when I realize that thirty-six thousand people will die today of malnutrition and its effects, in a world that could feed everyone. While the wealthy West eats and wastes its way to obesity, the poorest of the poor still starve to death. But no one has to die.

Faced with my personal sin and social complicity, it is entirely healthy to want to make amends. Doing so doesn't change God, but it does indicate to him, and more so to ourselves and others, that we want to take responsibility for what we have done and failed to do, and right our wrongs.

Apart from checking out all our penances with a trusted guide, three other sensible rules may assist. The first is to keep all penances positive, simple, and small.

While we may think our many and great sins demand great reparations—and in rare cases maybe they do—it's better to trust the effects of smaller acts of love done regularly. It shouldn't come as a surprise to discover that the two greatest Christian spiritual women of the twentieth century showed us the way. Both St. Teresa of Calcutta and Dorothy Day had great devotion to St. Thérèse of Lisieux's "little way," where everything is valued and no penance or act of love is considered unimportant. Something positive is always better than nothing. In contemporary spirituality, doing acts of love or charity are always to be preferred to hair shirts and flagellation.

The second sensible rule is to avoid the belief that we are too powerful or important to get down and get dirty. Again Mother Teresa and Dorothy Day observed that because personal power corrupts the human heart, we regularly need to have practical contact with "Jesus in a distressing disguise." This does not necessarily and only mean working in a soup kitchen or going to a third world country. It may mean visiting a loved one regularly in a nursing home, especially if the person doesn't even remember our name. Loneliness is one of the great poverties and distressing disguises in the world.

The third rule is to be aware that, because there is no sin we have ever committed for which God's mercy is not greater, our making amends is not about putting on a public or private show for God. Jesuit priest Frank Wallace wrote a book on prayer called *Encounter, Not Performance*, which about says it all. Most of us who find extra prayer, penance, and fasting difficult, both inside and outside the Lenten season, should remember that it is never about a performance that we think God will enjoy or will make him like us more. In fact, the more we put on a show for God, the more God must wonder why we are going through the routine. God's love and forgiveness is gratuitously and readily available to us. It is a question of claiming that, so as to live lives worthy of it.

Frank Wallace says that all acts of prayer and penance should be about an encounter with God: facing up to who we are, what we have done, and knowing that we are never defined by our most destructive behavior. Following the witness of St. Peter, who denied and abandoned the Lord, and St. Paul, who murdered Christ's followers, we simply have to be available to God and experience his loving presence in any way that helps us draw closer to the one who forgives and converts us to a new way of living.

Having invoked the sanity of the steps of AA earlier, maybe we should make its famous prayer our own as we make amends so that we might be changed into the people God intends:

> God grant me the sincerity to accept the things I
> cannot change.
> Courage to change the things I can
> And wisdom to know the difference.

Fasting: Appetites

As a priest, I have often had the honor of being invited into people's homes for a family meal. It is almost always a very enjoyable experience. Mind you, things have changed in many homes, and these days, when gathered at the table and invited to say grace before the meal, an assertive adolescent sometimes says, "Why are we saying grace? We never say grace. Why are you putting on a show for the priest?" To which I reply, "We are saying grace because sixteen thousand kids your age or younger will die today from no food, so we pray that this meal gives us the strength to make the world a more just place." I don't actually say that, but I really want to!

On another occasion, I was invited to a home for dinner. This family had been having more than a little trouble with their thirteen-year-old daughter, who was going through a particularly defiant and rebellious stage. The young girl was not happy with the vegetables her mother served at dinner and refused to eat them. The uneaten vegetables became the staging ground for an adolescent conflict. Trying to coax the girl into eating, her mother calmly used some lines I'd heard before: "Wasting food is a sin," and, "There are starving people in the world who would be grateful for what you don't want." With that, the girl jumped up and left the dining room. A few minutes later, she returned with an oversized envelope and a marker pen. She began to stuff the food into the envelope and as she did she angrily asked, "What starving people do you want me to send these vegetables to?" I can honestly say that celibacy was never a better option than at that moment!

If prayer and penance do not change an unchanging God, then neither does fasting. This multifaith, multicultural, and ancient practice is all about appetites—becoming aware of our wants on every level and making sure we are in control of them, and not the other way around.

Lenten fasts are not meant to be dietary, as good as it may be to lose a few pounds. A fast is aimed at enabling us to become aware of our hunger for God. The word *appetite*, comes from the Latin word *appetitus*, meaning "natural desire," so a fast is about regulation: minimizing our destructive desires and indulging those that bring us closer to light, to love, to God. For some, fasting from food is but one way to embody this process; for others fasting from abusive forms of pride, greed, envy, anger, lust, sloth, and power might be yet more fruitful. It is not by accident that the words *appetite* and *craving* are so closely linked. What is it we crave? Is the pursuing of it healthy for us and others? If not, then Lent is the time to fast so as to assert the self-control needed to unlock our craving's destructive grip on our desires.

In Lent, we have two mandated occasions for fast and abstinence: Ash Wednesday and Good Friday. In various parts of the world, there are many more, but these two are universally observed. For people between the ages of fourteen and sixty, we are asked to have only one major meal that day, and for that meal be without meat, so as to focus our mind, body, and spirit on the important season we are entering and on commemorating the day Jesus died. Although we must avoid the bad spirit's handiwork in scrupulosity, the nature of these days does not include a banquet of fine seafood.

The demand that we have two fast days from food makes more sense than ever before. Food is one of the narcotics of modern living. It doesn't take our pain away, but only dulls it for a while, and when it passes, our desolation returns with a vengeance.

Have you ever been on a cruise? If so, you know they are, for some, a journey to gluttony, where more is more. This is a trap and a serious mistake and not just because we pack on calories. It changes our mindset; our sense of entitlement can blind us to see our obligation to share with those who die every day because they have no food at all. This culture produces a thirteen-year-old middle-class kid who thinks that grace before meals is a formal and social nicety rather than the act of subversion that it is: "From everyone to whom much has been given, much will be required" (Luke 12:48).

Some of us have never truly been hungry, so it can be hard to appreciate fully how wasteful our developed world must appear to those who watch their families die of starvation. If fasting from food or anything else helps us to confront a world where people die each day because they lack food and clean water and the diseases this brings—by being mindful, changing our priorities, and calling for similar changes in the priorities of our nation, which spends more on bombs than starving babies—then we are not yet finished with this venerable practice.

"What starving people do you want me to send these vegetables to?" my thirteen-year-old friend asked. To which I wanted to reply, "Put your own name on the envelope because your own comfort makes you the neediest person in the world." By controlling our cravings, desires, appetites, and thirsts, it is hoped we come to rejoice also in seeing how life-giving the simple life actually is.

Lent is the season where we recommit to doing on earth what is done in heaven, where the hungry are welcomed and fed, the banquet of eternal joy and justice knows no end, and where the need to fast will be no more. But that day is yet to come.

Give Me Your Arms

The last of the corporal acts of mercy that we are encouraged to undertake in Lent is almsgiving, which more recently has been called works of charity. In AD 450, Pope St. Leo X is credited with having brought in this movement as one of the best ways to prepare for Easter. He argued that given that God held nothing back in generosity by giving us Christ, we therefore should hold nothing back in giving all we can to others. "No act of devotion on the part of the faithful gives God more pleasure than that which is lavished on his poor."

While St. Leo the Great knew that being with the poor, empowering them, and assisting them to be raised up was rarely an easy task, he taught that this work was not simply a one-way street, and that in turn God's poor had intangible but real gifts to offer the giver as well. He also made it clear that the best giving was done with a smile. "The giver of alms should be free from anxiety and full of joy." This disposition is far from the Christian woman in C.S. Lewis's *The Screwtape Letters* who went out and tracked down her charitable game. "She's the sort of woman who lives for others—you can tell the others by their hunted expression."

These days, we sometimes undergo an "exposure experience" to enable us to come face-to-face with stark material poverty, as a way of raising our consciousness about inequality and structural injustice, making us grateful for what we have, and making us aware of our grave obligations to make the world a better place for all God's children. Exposure experiences humanize human rights. Hopefully they enable people to become friends with those we want to help.

Most of us do not need to leave our own countries to find shocking economic deprivation. The wealthier our nation, the more confronting this is. However, it just so happens that my first dramatic exposure experience was not at home but abroad. St. Leo's teaching went from theory to practice in the Lent of 1990 with extraordinary results.

My provincial sent me to a Jesuit Communications Conference in Asia in March, 1990. It was held in Manila, the Philippines, and the theme of the conference was "Media at the Service of Poor." In the preparatory material, I read that we would be spending the first few days as guests in a community where we would be exposed to great poverty. I was anxious about how I would cope, and that proved to be the perfect response.

Within twenty-four hours of arriving in a hot and humid Manila, I was told that I would be living for four days near Smokey Mountain, where I would be hosted by a family. It was impossible for me to stay with the family on Smokey Mountain because the government forbade foreigners to do so, and in any case, the family had no room. So I slept on the floor of the local parish church and visited from sunrise to sunset.

I had never heard of Smokey Mountain. It no longer exists, having been closed down in 1995. For over forty years, it was home to nearly thirty thousand people who lived upon two million metric tons of waste. It was the rubbish dump for metro Manila and the residents became a scavenging community, sorting through the daily dumps of garbage for anything to eat, recycle, or resell. It got its name from the smoldering fire that was at the core of the mountain of rubbish. Sometimes a noxious vapor would emerge with horrible health consequences in an already unspeakable human habitat. The community lived on three sides of the mountain. The fourth side was a canal over which there were makeshift communal semipublic toilets and showers that dropped away to the side of the hill. There was no sanitation, anywhere.

Nothing prepared me for Smokey Mountain. I smelt it before I saw it, and when I saw it, I couldn't believe it. The crest of the hill was indeed billowing smoke, and running water was only available at public pumps. Homes were made of every weather-resistant material imaginable.

On arrival, I met the local Jesuits who looked after the Smokey Mountain parish. They were campaigning to have the dump shut down. The parish priest immediately took me to meet the family who had adopted me during my stay. As a white Westerner in these parts, I stood out as an exotic creature. There were children everywhere— dirty, energetic, scavenging children. Soon they were following me and wanting to hold my hand and touch my clean clothes. Why did I wear a bright white shirt? It made me as obvious as I looked.

We had to circle one side of the mountain, which enabled me to see the canal, the public bathrooms, and public water pumps. My head started pounding, maybe from the effect of the smoking fumes as much as the assault on all my senses. And then on finding a small narrow laneway, we started the climb to Bing's home. As we walked between the packed-in dwellings, my heart was close to breaking; my stomach was dry retching.

When I arrived at Bing's neatly kept home, I was given a warm welcome. Spontaneously Bing's small children all flung their arms around me. There are many responses to desperate situations, and flight and fight are among two of the most common. I wanted to take flight—immediately!

Bing saw that I was very hot and bothered by my new surroundings and offered me a drink of water. I had an ethical dilemma: how far was I prepared to share in the life of the poor? All I could think of were the diseases I could catch from drinking water from the pump. As thirsty as I was, I declined the offer, knowing that later I would privately gulp down one of the bottles of water in my backpack. I watched as Bing's son, Boy, served glasses on a tray. As we talked about his family and his life on Smokey Mountain, I felt a fraud, justifying to myself that it was sensible to avoid any waterborne diseases, while also knowing that I was only comfortable when my heroic commitment to the poor was on my terms.

A few minutes later, Boy emerged with a large sealed bottle of water and a sealed plastic glass. I was offered water again and Boy put the sealed plastic cup in my hand. On seeing these more sanitary provisions, I had a change of mind and accepted the water. Flushed with embarrassment, I may have found my thirst again, but I was left spiritually as parched as a desert. In every single home I visited on Smokey Mountain over the next four days, I was always offered sealed bottles of water, plastic-clad cups, and lots of hugs.

Because of the centrality of the image of the desert during Lent, images of thirst and water are omnipresent too. In one of the years of Lent, it comes into clear relief when we hear about Jesus and the woman at the well. At that famous well, Jesus enters the world of a poor Samaritan woman who has been dumped five times by the men who married her. By asking for a drink, by engaging her in conversation, by understanding her situation, and offering a way out of the cycle of emotional abuse in which she was caught, Jesus gives her the greatest gift of all: personal dignity. This changes her life and turns her into one of the earliest missionaries in the Gospel of John.

Although separated by time and space, a drink of water helped a Samaritan woman and me confront the embarrassment of our worlds, our quick and inaccurate judgments, and reassess the choices that could lead us to life. Recognizing that no matter how good the gift of water was that day, the unknown and unexpected giver of the gift for both of us was so much greater.

Bing and his wife died too early of natural deaths, due, no doubt, from the stark poverty of their community. But in the end, almsgiving won the day. Through Caritas and Catholic Charities, Boy and his four siblings learned to read and write through the programs run at the local Catholic parish. None of Bing's family now lives in a slum. Boy went on to become a chef and now works at an international hotel in Manila. All his kids are in school, and their apartment has clean running water.

Pope St. Leo X was right in saying that true acts of Lenten charity, corporal acts of mercy, are among the best ways to prepare for Easter, marked as they should be by a generous exchange of gifts. The word *corporal* comes from the Latin word *corpus*, meaning "the body." The body is the point of commitment. A corporal work of mercy, therefore, is an act of incarnated love and compassion. It's all about where we put our bodies. Even if it takes a while, the gift of life and joy that should characterize the way and the nature of our giving is always best when it is more about giving our arms then simply giving alms.

TRANSFIGURATION

Changed from Glory into Glory

*O*f all the great hymns the Wesley brothers wrote —and there are many of them—for me the greatest is "Love divine, all loves excelling." Written by Charles in 1747, the third verse is among the finest Christian poetry I know:

Finish then thy new creation,
Pure and sinless let us be;
Let us see thy great salvation,
Perfectly restored in thee:
Changed from glory into glory,
Till in heav'n we take our place,
Till we cast our crowns before thee,
Lost in wonder, love and praise.

The phrase *changed from glory into glory* has puzzled some commentators. I am not one of them, echoing as it does St. Irenaeus's famous line: "The glory of God is humanity fully alive." At our best, when we are faithful, hopeful, and loving, we are already, albeit imperfectly, reflections of God's glory. And as St. Paul knew, there was even greater glory yet to be revealed *to* us and *in* us (cf. Rom 8:18 and Col 3:4).

The pivotal story during the forty days of Lent is the transfiguration, which is all about God's glory revealed in and through Jesus. It's the bridge that gets us from the starkness of the Lenten desert and moves us on to the abundance of the Easter garden. While each of the evangelists use the details of this event to draw particular theological points, all of them brilliantly hold together the divinity and the humanity of Jesus.

In recent years, the Church has accentuated Jesus' humanity. We can see why. For a long period, the divine nature of Christ was sometimes so overemphasized that some people spoke as if Jesus were a divine being just parading around in human form. That's a heresy. Jesus was fully and truly human. With the advent of the biblical movement throughout the twentieth century, we recovered the equally important human nature of Christ. But there can be a danger in overemphasizing this as well, where Christ is seen as a good, noble, and sacrificial man, but simply one of us. That's a heresy. Jesus was fully and truly divine.

The transfiguration event holds both equal natures of Christ in tension. All the accounts tell us that Jesus was metamorphosed before the eyes of the three disciples. At Tabor, Jesus' divine nature was seen directly and immediately by them, which is why this feast was once called the "Manifestation of Divine Glory." Trying to describe the indescribable, the evangelists use the shorthand of the Old

Testament to set the scene: a mountaintop religious experience, a cloud that covers the actors, and the glory of God revealed through dazzling light. Jesus is even joined by the greatest of all Jewish patriarchs, all of whom encountered God's glory on a mountain: Abraham, Moses, and Elijah.

However, the evangelists also brilliantly draw out the humanity of Jesus at the end of this dazzling spiritual display. Just when Peter, James, and John (who mirror on earth the heavenly Abraham, Moses, and Elijah) want to stay on Mount Tabor, they have to come down the mountain, and start another journey with Jesus to another mountain—Calvary. They have to walk with Jesus to his very human death.

There are differences, especially between Moses on Sinai and Jesus on Tabor, that reveal even more how Lent can enable us to change from glory into glory. Moses goes up the mountain alone, whereas Jesus takes companions who share in the experience and witness it. The face of God is hidden from Moses, whereas on Tabor, Jesus is given to us as the face of God for the world. On Sinai, Moses receives a code of law and is told to make sure the people obey it. On Tabor, Jesus receives a proclamation of God's love and we're told to listen to him. While Moses' face shines, Jesus' whole body is transfigured with light. Moses descends to enforce the law; Jesus comes down to die that we might live.

Furthermore, Jesus does not change because of the experience on Tabor. He remains authoritative, compassionate, and forgiving. The change occurs in the three disciples. They know that to behold the glory of God, they don't need a mountaintop light show. They discover the divinity of Jesus in his humanity, through the uncompromised and uncompromising love of the world's only complete human being. One early commentator said that Christ's transfiguration was like the opening out of a beautiful rose. The transformation happens more in the one who beholds its unfolding majesty than in the rose itself.

And so, what does this mean for us in Lent? We don't have to feel cheated because we have no access to Jesus in the same way Peter, James, and John did. Nor do we have to keep looking for our own version of Mount Tabor, as good as religious experiences are. What we need is an ever-deepening faith to believe that the glory of God is fully and totally revealed in God's own Son, Jesus of Nazareth.

The transfiguration is not just a once-off event for Jesus alone. Jesus' glory is soon going to be further revealed in a dramatically different way: in his being lifted up on the cross of death. What holds Tabor and Calvary together is love. So often, we hear people say they have not, or cannot, experience the glory or presence of God, and therefore they deny that God exists. Tabor and Calvary show us that if we want to encounter God, then we have to give and receive love. This is not an optional extra for the Christian life. As St. John says in his letter, "Those who say, 'I love God,' and hate their brothers or sisters, are liars" (1 John 4:20).

The problem with the concept of love is that we've devalued the currency. We say it too often about things we don't or can't love. We say "I love you" to people we don't love, and because we've learned that actions are more telling than words, we don't easily believe others when they tell us they love us. We can feel unlovable and cynical about the whole experience.

But this Lent, there are three things of which we can be sure:

- If we feel distant from God, we only have to guess who has moved away from whom. Nothing we do stops God from loving us.
- God loves us as we are, not as we would like to be. As the old saying goes, "You don't have to get good to get God, you have to get God to try and get good."
- Finally, as the song sings, "You ain't nobody 'til somebody loves ya."

So for us, being vulnerable enough to tell those we love that we love them is no sentimental exercise, but a participation in the heart of God. The Father told the world of his love for the Son on Tabor. By taking the risk of professing our sincere love, others may clearly hear the voice of God though us, and we may discover ourselves transfigured by the personal love of God. In the process, God may move from being an idea, an abstraction, even an object of curiosity, to the focus of a loving experience that can give our lives meaning, purpose, and hope. The transfiguration sets the pattern for all of us to hear the Father say to each of us through Christ, "You are my son. You are my daughter—and I love you," and to take up our Christian mission given to us at our baptisms—to take up our cross, and follow Christ to the glory of his resurrection.

As we move to Easter, let's ascend the mountaintop together, experience the power of God's absolute and unconditional love and so be "changed from glory into glory, Till in heav'n we take our place, Till we cast our crowns before thee, Lost in wonder, love and praise."

PALM SUNDAY

Processing into Love

*A*s a child, I can remember our diocese having large processions for the Feasts of Corpus Christi, Christ the King, and one of the Marian feast days. They were called "public demonstrations of Catholic faith." For children, they were long and boring, but they did give us a sense that we belonged to something big, and someone bigger, and that our faith had a "stand up and be counted" dimension to it.

For many Catholics today, large-scale religious processions are quickly becoming a thing of the past. That's unfortunate! Maybe World Youth Day for young adults presently provides a similar experience. These occasions are "event dramas," and Palm Sunday commemorates one of the greatest of events, and is among the most dramatic of them. Even the name of this feast tells us some of the tension in the story: "Palm Sunday of the Lord's Passion."

Before the Second Vatican Council, there were two feasts, Palm Sunday on the First Sunday of Lent and Passion Sunday on the Sixth Sunday of Lent, the Sunday immediately before Easter Sunday. The former one (Palm Sunday) was moved into the latter one (Passion Sunday) in the 1960s. The feast we commemorate holds in tension both the palms and the passion together. It's not one *or* the other.

Even the congregation's posture tells us how different this day is. There are only two mandated congregational processions left in the Missal to be observed throughout the entire Church: one for Palm Sunday, and the other to the Altar of Repose on Holy Thursday. On Palm Sunday, we recall Jesus' procession into Jerusalem. However, this procession is not meant to be a historical pageant. Like all liturgical moments, it's meant to intersect with our own lives and speak to our journey of faith.

What makes this procession so powerful is that it starts with hysteria and ends in death. And that tells us something we need to hear. This is also the only Sunday where we read two Gospels: one of false adulation and the other one of false accusation.

The accounts of the passion tell us that by the week's end, the local crowd was unable to recognize Jesus because he didn't fit their expectations of the Messiah. The crowd in Jerusalem receives him like a pop star, acclaiming him as their own. By Good Friday, the chief priests and elders manipulate the crowd's enthusiasm to force Pilate to execute Jesus. And throughout it all—during the adulation of the crowd, their change of allegiance to Barabbas, and at his trial—Jesus hardly says a word. Jesus' silence is deafening!

In our journey of faith, we should always be on guard against being part of a manipulated crowd. The unchecked enthusiasms of a crowd can carry us away to places, people, or things we would not ordinarily choose and should not embrace. If we are vulnerable, then a gifted guru, through his or her version of eternal life, can whip us into a spiritual frenzy. We only have to look at the power of the media and advertising to see how susceptible we are to fashionable ideologies, dress codes, and what and who is in or out. Every time we buy something, because someone else has it or because we convince ourselves that our wants are really our needs, the crowd has won. The story of Passion Sunday is that the manipulation of a crowd, even by legitimate authorities, can be the beginning of spiritual death. Hype often distorts priorities, blurs good judgment, and chooses expediency over integrity.

The liturgical movement of the assembly and the emotions of Palm Sunday brilliantly enshrine this when we process from the cries of adulation of Palm Sunday to the derision of Good Friday with frightening ease.

We can be a fickle and unpredictable lot. One well-known example demonstrates this point. I was studying in London when Diana, Princess of Wales, died. I stood in the Mall for her funeral procession. It was an extraordinary experience. But if ever we needed convincing just how fickle we are, all we had to recall was, that only two weeks before, the same people now claiming her as "queen of our hearts" had bought thousands of papers and magazines with headlines like "Diana, Say No to Dodi"; "Soap-Opera Queen Flees England to Be with Muslim Lover"; and "Diana: Dodi Will Not Do." Talk radio was full of it too, with most callers telling us that Diana was mentally ill, spoiled, a scheming temptress, or a disgrace to all things British.

The death of a thirty-six-year-old mother of two is always an immense tragedy. But who could have predicted that the crowd could literally change its mind over one Paris night, and come to see that Diana was one of the greatest English women ever, and that her passing would be an occasion for national grief, the like of which that nation had never seen.

I will never forget the solemnity of the crowd as Diana's casket went on its way to the abbey. Millions were eerily quiet, reverent, and maybe feeling a little guilty. On Diana's trip away from the abbey, the crowd cheered, threw flowers, and applauded. It was Palm Sunday in reverse. The Jerusalem crowd threw branches and cheered first, and then watched the death march in shameful silence later.

Processions matter. The point of religious processions is not just about getting us from one location in the church to the next. They also mark a rite of passage. Think of all the smaller, informal, and nonmandatory processions most Christians undertake in their lives: to the baptismal font, down the aisle to take their marriage vows, to graduate from a school or college, to be professed or ordained, and to be farewelled in the rite of Christian burial. In each case, we recess out of the Church differently from how we entered it: as a newly initiated member of the Christian community, as a husband or wife, as a graduate, as a religious or a priest, and to be buried or cremated.

On the first Palm Sunday, and every one since, we should recess out of this feast differently from the way we processed into it because we hear proclaimed three extraordinary and life-changing things:

- Jesus knows what it's like to be heralded on Sunday and condemned on Friday,
- Jesus loved us so much that he laid down his own life so that we might live, and
- Jesus showed us that the price of walking on palm branches is in the taking up of the cross.

How do we prepare for all the Calvarys of our world, and be Christlike? How do we face our personal passions?

Let's start with what Jesus did in his passion:

- he healed the ear of the High Priest's servant,
- he spoke the truth to Pilate,
- he empathized with the women of Jerusalem,
- he forgave those who condemned him, and
- he had compassion toward the other criminals being crucified.

As we physically and spiritually process into Holy Week, we may live in a similar way:

- walking away from inflicting pain to being a healer,
- desisting with lies and speaking the truth in love,
- resisting the temptation to judge, and embracing empathy as our first response, and

- being generous always and everywhere with forgiveness and compassion.

Healing, truthfulness, empathy, forgiveness, and compassion. No more and no less is asked of us if we are to follow the one of whom we sing at the start of this holiest of weeks, "Lord of earth, sky and sea. King of Love on Calvary."[9]

HOLY THURSDAY

Getting Down and Dirty

*T*he verses of a well-known African American spiritual run, "Let us break bread...drink wine... praise God together on our knees." These verses finish, "When I fall on my knees with my face to the rising sun, O Lord, have mercy on me." Some versions, even more poignantly for Holy Week, have the line, "When I fall on my knees with my face to the *rising Son*, O Lord, have mercy on me."

The earliest name the Christians gave to the Eucharist was *the breaking of the bread*. In the most ancient description of the Eucharist in the New Testament, St. Paul says in the First Letter to the Corinthians that he is handing on what he received: that to share in the Lord's Supper we must break the bread and drink the cup. In the story of the disciples on the road to Emmaus, they only recognize Jesus when, at journey's end, while at table, the bread is broken. And in the Acts of the Apostles, we're told several times how the earliest Christians gathered in one another's homes for the breaking of the bread.

Whatever else the Eucharist meant to the earliest Church, the action of breaking apart and pouring out captured how Jesus was present to them in the meal he left them. Although these days other terms like *Mass* and *Eucharist* are much more frequently used for our sacred ritual of Word and Sacrament, to this day, the liturgy maintains a connection with this heritage in the *fractio panis*, "the breaking of the bread," during which we sing the Lamb of God.

If Easter is to come alive, then we too have to be prepared to be broken and poured out in love for our world. No wonder St. Augustine said in the fifth century, "Become what you see, and receive what you are."[10] It's not just the static presence of Christ we're asked to imitate, but the challenge to enter into his activity of sacrificial love. Every time we come forward and receive communion, we say "Amen" to Jesus Christ as body broken and blood poured out. In doing so, we reaffirm that this is how far God went to show his love for us. This is also the intimate moment where God meets us in the most broken parts of our lives and in the times we feel completely poured out. God is a companion in our suffering and sacrifices. In turn, Holy Thursday shows us how we should live. Everyone who receives Christ in communion says they are prepared to pay the price of being one with him in being broken and poured out in love for the world.

Breaking and pouring, however, are but two of the four actions given to us by Jesus on Holy Thursday. The other two are washing and sending. John's Gospel has no recounting of the meal, but goes into great detail about Jesus' service. He knew how intimately interconnected all these are. It is what we do away from the Eucharist that indicates how seriously we take what we do at it. At the end of every Mass we are told to go out to "love and serve the Lord." Even the term *Mass* comes from the Latin word *missa*, meaning "to be sent."

By taking up Jesus' commission to serve, we show how his life, death, and resurrection continue to "Easter in us" and change the world for good. As a result of that first Holy Thursday, there is no service too small, no act of kindness too insignificant, and no moment of love inconsequential in our service of Christ's kingdom. We are people who look for opportunities to take up the commission to serve all those who feel spent with the brokenness of their lives.

In organizing the Holy Thursday liturgy over the years, I have discovered that not everyone likes the small act of humble service we do in the washing of the feet. Several years ago I invited Jeremy, the chairman of our parish council, to have his feet washed on Holy Thursday. "Absolutely not!" Jeremy snapped back, which was not his usual style. "Look, I'm sorry," he went on, "but I find that whole thing appalling: bare feet, water, and wiping. It's all disgusting. And I saw you kiss the foot of someone last year. It might've been fine for Jesus to get down and dirty in first-century Palestine, but not here and now. I can barely watch this ritual, let alone be part of it."

I felt like saying, "Jeremy, don't hold back! Tell me what you're really thinking!"

Jeremy of course has a valid point. The washing of guest's feet may have been a custom in Jesus' day, but it is foreign to Western societies today. Mind you, don't tell that to anyone who pays good money for a foot massage at a day spa!

Because we are unacquainted with this most important practice, we can miss the significance of one of the most important points in John's account. In Jesus' day, a Jewish host certainly *never* washed his guests' feet. Indeed, in most houses not even Jewish servants performed this act. It was the task of the least in the house, one for the Gentile, or non-Jewish, servant. No wonder Peter objects to it being done to him by Jesus. And the household codes tell us that it was not done regularly, but only on those occasions where guests who had completed a long trip were received into a home at journey's end.

By doing this act, then, Jesus announces the end of the road for weary travelers. For him and his disciples, the journey, which they had embarked upon together years before, was now about to take a final turn, indeed it was to be a definitive rite of passage. But given that Jesus had also preached that anyone who wants to be first, must be last of all and servant of all, then in the action of a slave, he walks the talk, and does the job of the lowliest person in the house.

I've always been struck by Jeremy's words: "It might've been fine for Jesus to get down and dirty in first-century Palestine, but not here and now." I don't want to hold Jeremy out to dry, as though his response was odd or wrong. I had the very same reaction as him on seeing a religious act of love last year. On November 6, 2013, when Pope Francis was on "walkabout" after his General Audience, he came across fifty-three-year-old Vinicio Riva.

Vinicio suffers from neurofibromatosis, the disease made famous in the film *The Elephant Man*.

What happened next? Pope Francis immediately got down from the popemobile, embraced and kissed Vinicio, prayed with him, and blessed him.

I'm ashamed to say that when I saw these images, I knew I would not be able to do what Pope Francis had done. Ritual washing of the feet is one thing; kissing Vinicio would be quite another. But here

was the best lesson I've had on what the Lord did at the Last Supper.

Welcome to Holy Thursday, where God, revealed to us in Jesus Christ, says there is not a part of any of us that is untouchable, that is beyond God's loving embrace—not one part. This is when our God gets "down and gets dirty" so that we can rise up to claim our dignity as Christ's disciples, following his lead, and where we commit ourselves again to acts of loving service that set other people free.

"For I have set you an example, that you also should do as I have done to you" (John 13:15). Hearing this and saying it is one thing, living it is quite another. Thank God,

Jesus also gave us the Eucharist to sustain us in our service where we can move away from shame, claim our dignity, and serve others so they might be set free in the same way our faith liberates us.

We are not sure of the origins of "Let us break bread together on our knees." We do know that the members of the African American community that composed the spiritual were slaves; they were the lowliest in the house, and needed to affirm their hope in the face of institutionalized evil. In following Jesus' example of being broken and poured out in love, may our service in his name enable us to see the face of the Rising Son as we serve God together on our knees.

From Exile We Return

In a profound poem, French Jesuit Didier Rimaud makes a stark, telling, and correct connection between our celebration of the Eucharist and our liberation begun in the story of the exodus. The church does the same thing twice during the Easter Triduum. On Holy Thursday, as we remember the first Eucharist, we always begin by reading about the first Passover. They're intimately linked. For Christians, the freedom gained by the chosen people in Egypt was consummated in the freedom embodied in the life, death, and resurrection of Jesus.

> In remembrance of you,
> We take the bread of Easter in our hands,
> This bread do we consume:

It does no longer taste of bitter herbs,
  nor of unleavened bread.
It is the bread of a land promised us
  where we shall be set free.

In remembrance of you,
We drink the wine of Easter at our feast,
This wine do we hold dear:
It does no longer taste of bitter springs,
  nor of dark salty pools.
It is the wine of a land promised us
  where we shall be made whole.

In remembrance of you,
From exile we return!
In remembrance of you,
We walk across the sea![11]

The Passover and resulting exodus are *the* defining
moments in the history of Israel. However, for Christians
they can be distant events that happened to "the Jews," and
of little consequence for us today. On two levels, however,
the exodus should be a defining moment in our lives too.

On the first level, as Christians we look to Jesus for
salvation. His personal and religious identity was inextri-
cably and proudly caught up with the Passover and the
exodus. This is one of the reasons why it is patently absurd
for a Christian to be anti-Jewish. Such Christians end up
hating the very religious tradition that formed Jesus, his
mother and St. Joseph, as well as all the apostles. If God
chose our Jewish brothers and sisters as the people from

whom the Lord would come, who are we to declare him mistaken? One of the worst things Christianity has done to the memory of Jesus is to strip him of his religious heritage. This has terrible consequences. If we are sincere about getting to know the historical Jesus, then it helps to have some devoutly Jewish friends to guide us.

On another level, the Passover and exodus are now metaphors for what God does through Christ in all of our lives. Many of us know what it is like to be stuck. Imprisoned by our body, mind, or soul—these places can be very dark indeed. In the midst of the splendor of our Holy Thursday liturgy, let's remember that the Passover in Egypt, and the Last Supper upon which it is based, were celebrated in the most desolate of circumstances. The Israelites were in exile and enslaved. Jesus was on the eve of his passion and death. The Israelites and Jesus held on to the hope, first, that they would be freed from bondage, and second, that God would remain faithful. For the Israelites, their hope led to the exodus. For Jesus, his hope and trust led to the resurrection.

But there is one dramatic and important difference between the Passover and the Last Supper. The Israelite's freedom cost many lives in Egypt, the firstborn son of every Egyptian family. It is a murderous story. By contrast, not one life was directly lost in the wake of the resurrection. In fact, the opposite is true; it gave all people the opportunity to know eternal life. God was so despairing of human death and the never-ending cycle of violence within which we were caught that Jesus went to his death so that death would be no more.

The gospel shows us how those who follow Jesus can

break this cycle of destruction—we must serve one another, even our enemies. We get down on the floor and assume the nature of a slave so that others might discover their human dignity and worth. In doing so, we discover a wonderful paradox: by expressing our love for others in acts of goodness, service, and kindness, we are not diminished, but enhanced.

Some people want to reduce the institution of the Eucharist to simply adoring Christ in the Blessed Sacrament. That is a good, holy, and right element to Holy Thursday, but it is not the only one. We are not just called to adore Christ at the altar of repose, but to process away from it and be Christ in the world. We have to make the connection between Christ's service and hospitality in our day-to-day lives. If Holy Thursday has any impact on us, then it should leave us conscious of the injustices in the world and should give us a desire to want to work for the liberation of all people everywhere.

Pedro Arrupe, the former leader of the Jesuits, said in his address at the Eucharistic Congress in Philadelphia in 1976,

> If there is hunger anywhere in the world, then our celebration of the Eucharist is somehow incomplete everywhere in the world....In the Eucharist we receive Christ hungering in the world. He comes to us, not alone, but with the poor, the oppressed, the starving of the earth. Through him they are looking to us for help, for justice, for love expressed in action. Therefore we cannot properly receive the Bread of life unless at the

same time we give the bread of life to those in need wherever and whoever they may be.

There are often two blocks that prevent us from doing this. The first block is that when we start working on the world's problems we believe that our efforts won't make much of a difference. The reason we bother with our work for justice that flows from the Lord's Supper is not because it makes us feel good. It's because it's what Jesus did for us. He gave us the Eucharist, this meal for saints and sinners, where we gain the strength to be Christ in the way we make the world ridiculously hospitable and radically just.

Holy Thursday gives us "food for the journey" so that we can return from our exile and walk across the sea, even as we taste the bitter herbs and the dark salty pools of the world's injustice. The service and hospitality of the Eucharist establishes the pattern of our daily lives, remembering that, by journey's end, we will, in Christ, inherit the land promised us, where all creation will be made whole, and we will be set free.

GOOD FRIDAY

A Mother's Only Child

On Good Friday in recent years, I have undertaken a process of becoming someone in the story, seeing and feeling the drama from their point of view. Apart from walking with Christ, without question the next most powerful person to feel with on Good Friday is Mary, the mother of Jesus. We know from every Gospel that she accompanied her only child to his death. What must it have been like for her to watch her innocent child condemned, tortured, and capitally punished by the state? What must it be like now to be a faithful parent in the face of the tragic death of your child? Mary provides a way into fidelity in the face of utter powerlessness, of trusting that some good, any good, might ever emerge from evil, and that the hope of Easter Sunday can be born from the darkness of Good Friday.

Rather than reflect on a mother's love and grief in the abstract, what follows is a Good Friday story in the here and now.

My first appointment as a deacon and then a priest was at St. Canice's Parish in Kings Cross, Sydney. Kings Cross is that city's red-light district. The Jesuits have cared for this parish since 1989. In my time, the rectory received an average of fifty-six callers a day. It was one of the few parish houses where the clergy did not need to leave the house to go to bed tired. At 4:00 on a Monday morning in Lent, there was an urgent ringing of the front doorbell. Halfway down the stairs, I called out more loudly than anticipated, "Oh give it a break; I'm coming!" The doorbell ringing ceased.

When I opened the door, I found a hysterical woman slumped on the top step. I found out later she was twenty-eight years of age, though she looked fifty-eight. Life had not been kind to her. When she could catch her breath, she told me she wanted to get into the church. She looked as though she could be stoned on drugs, but my intuition told me to go with it. She followed me. I opened up the church and turned on the lights. As I did, the young woman ran all the way down the aisle to the high altar and stood in front of the tabernacle and screamed the most primal scream I have ever heard. After I calmed her down sufficiently to sit with me on the front pew, she kept repeating like a mantra, "Sebastian's dead. Sebastian's dead.…" I found that her name was Jenny and that she went to give her six-month-old son, Sebastian, his feed at 2:00 a.m. "He wasn't breathing properly, so I took him to the hospital." I still wondered if Jenny was in fact on a trip. "Where is Sebastian now?" I asked. "At St. Vincent's," she replied. St. Vincent's was our wonderful, local public hospital run by the Sisters of Charity. It did not treat children. Adults only. So now I could test my hallucination theory. "Why don't we go back there now?" To which Jenny looked up, took me by the hand, and said, "I'll go back there with you." We walked to the neighboring suburb with Jenny gently sobbing all the way. On walking into the Accident and Emergency Department at St. V's, and through the large plate glass window, Mary McGuire, the night charge nurse and one of our parishioners, came running out, "Oh Father, thank God you have brought her back." And with that she ushered us inside. "She arrived here at 2:30 a.m. this morning with a blue baby," Mary explained. "She said the child wasn't breathing very well. The little boy had been dead for hours. She wanted us to resuscitate the baby, and we explained that we couldn't and why. Then she became so upset, she jumped up and fled into the night. We don't have a name or an address or a date of birth for the baby or for the mother. We have called the police to see if they can find her. We are fairly sure it is a SIDS death, but the child is now a coroner's case."

In fact, what happened to Jenny is extraordinary. Understandably devastated at the death of her baby son, she started aimlessly wandering the streets of Kings Cross, and by 3:30 a.m., she ended up on a park bench with Con, the then most famous homeless man in the red-light district and our leading Catholic parishioner. Con came to everything at the church, but more eagerly anticipated the food that almost always followed. He listened to Jenny's tragic story and shared his whiskey bottle with her until he declared at 3:50 a.m., "I can't help you, but I know people who can." It was a homeless alcoholic man who brought a grieving mother to the rectory door at 4:00 a.m. It was Con who was urgently ringing the front doorbell until he heard me call out. Then he said to Jenny, "I stole a candlestick from this lot last week and hocked it. They don't like me much at present. I'm pissin' off. You're on your own." Hence, I opened the door to find Jenny and no Con.

When I got Jenny back to the rectory, not only did I hear the story of what had happened to her that morning, but I got her backstory too. She was a woman in prostitution who lived with her physically, sexually, and emotionally violent partner, Greg, who was also her pimp. Greg was Sebastian's father. He had ordered a DNA test to make sure. Jenny and Greg were substance abusers and alcoholics.

To say I was pastorally in over my head would be a gross understatement. By 6:30 a.m., I did not have a clue what to do next, and then I recalled that Mary McGuire had said that the staff thought Sebastian was a SIDS death. I don't know why or how I knew that the local SIDS Association had an emergency help line, but I thank God to this day that I did. I found it and called it, and the very reassuring woman at the other end of the phone said they would send out someone as soon as possible.

You never know when one of your best friends is about to walk into your life. At 8:00 a.m., Annie McNamara walked through the rectory door and in doing so she, her wonderful husband Johnny, and their loving family walked into my life. Johnny, a medical doctor, and Annie, a registered nurse, had lost Monica, their second eldest daughter to SIDS. One of the ways they dealt with their grief at that time was to volunteer with the SIDS Association for other families going through the same tragedy. Seeing Annie and Jenny talk to each other was a lesson in like-to-like counselling. Annie could touch and console Jenny in a way that I could never have been capable of doing.

By 11:00 a.m., Jenny told us she did not want to go back to Greg. I found her a bed in a church-run women's refuge perfectly named: Mana House. Annie and I accompanied Jenny back to her apartment to get necessities for a couple of days. On the top floor of the worst apartment building in one of the worst parts of town there was Jenny at her front door, then Annie and then me on the stairs. As Jenny went to put the key in the door, she turned to Annie and me and said, "I hope Greg hasn't still got the shotgun." "What shotgun would that be?" I inquired. This was the first we had heard of a shotgun. "This morning, Greg accused me of having killed Sebastian, so he got the shotgun out to kill me." I have never considered myself much of a martyr, but even I knew that the mother of six in front of me should not be the next person to follow Jenny into Greg's potential shooting range. I was so brave that I hardly recognized myself! I pushed Annie out of the way and followed Jenny into the apartment.

This apartment was one of the most miserable human habitats I have ever seen in my life; actually it is the stench I remember most. And in the corner of this open-plan room was Greg and the shotgun. He was stark naked and spread-eagled on his double bed dead to the world asleep—drunk, stoned, or both (at least that was what I was hoping). Now I have seen enough episodes of

CSI to know that I had to "secure the scene," so I went over to the bed, picked up the gun, and carried it to the opposite corner of the room and piled clothes upon it. Greg stirred, but didn't wake. Meanwhile, I went and joined Annie and Jenny on the enclosed balcony of the apartment, which was the nursery. It was a tale of two rooms. While one was not fit for dignified human living, the nursery was neat and clean. Everything was labeled and there were little stuffed panda bears. It smelled sweet. These rooms told the story of what Jenny loved and the life she hated.

Sebastian's autopsy took six days, and in that time, Annie and I gained Jenny's trust sufficiently for her to tell us her complex story, so much so that she asked me to contact her parents, from whom she had been estranged for five years. They were decent, hardworking people in the neighboring state, who, by Jenny's own admission, did nothing to her that might explain how their only child got into drugs, ran away from home, and later became involved in prostitution. "I can't talk to them, but you tell them what's happened and where I am." Vera and Jack were initially delighted to hear that their daughter was alive and relatively well, but this phone conversation became excruciatingly painful for all of us when I explained that the grandson they never knew they had had died six days ago. The rest of the tragic tale of Jenny's life could wait. They said they would fly down to be reunited with Jenny as soon as they could.

That same day, the body was released to the undertakers. There were no suspicious circumstances. The cause of death was "most likely SIDS." The next day, Jenny asked Annie and me to take her to the funeral home to see Sebastian for the last time. Jack and Vera were flying in that night. The funeral was scheduled thirty-six hours after they arrived. It was confronting to walk into the viewing room of the funeral parlor and find an open white casket. They had done a wonderful job on Sebastian; he just looked as though he was asleep. Jenny asked me to say some prayers and then asked Annie and me if she could be alone with her baby for the last time. "Of course you can," said Annie with all the empathy and support within her. We went and sat with the receptionist in the foyer. After ten minutes, Annie said, "I'll just go and see if she is okay." From down the corridor to the viewing rooms I heard Annie screaming. Racing to the door, I found Jenny on the floor. She had taken Sebastian out of the casket, laid down on the floor, and with her baby in her left arm, she mainlined a syringe of heroin into her neck. She was committing suicide. Annie kept her awake and alert. I raced back to the receptionist. At times, there is often a black humor moment in situations like this. When I told her, "You have to call the ambulance. She's dying in that room. She's committing suicide," the receptionist jumped up and yelled out, "Oh my God! No one has ever died here before!" No, I thought, they usually come that way. The ambulance was there within minutes. Jenny was given narcaine, and she came around. We spent the rest of the day at the hospital until I talked the medicos into releasing her into my care rather than into an involuntary admission in the psychiatric unit. She had her child's funeral to attend in the morning. Annie had to go home to care for her family.

Vera and Jack rang to say they had arrived at a Sydney hotel. Jenny asked me to accompany her to their hotel room and help her explain her situation. On speaking and seeing their daughter for the first time in five years, they had to touch their grief for a grandchild (their only one) they didn't know they had and find out that Jenny was a woman in prostitution, had an addiction to drugs and alcohol, and that day had attempted suicide. How do you start to take any of this onboard? Jack and Vera were salt-of-the-earth people, and they were about to become lights to the world. What did they do with the enormity of devastating news that now confronted them? They focused on the one positive thing they could—they had been reunited with their child. The story of the prodigal son had never been more real to me than at that moment as I left Jenny with her parents that night.

Days before, when we were planning Sebastian's funeral service at St. Canice's, Jenny had asked for only three things: "I Will Always Love You" by Whitney Houston; one of his panda bears next to the little white casket; and the only hymn she remembered from Sunday school— "Amazing Grace." We had all three. Vera supported Jenny as though she had never left their side. Greg sat in the back row, without the shotgun. When the time came for Jenny to follow her baby's casket out of the church, she marched past it with the angriest and most defiant walk I have ever seen in my life. She rejected all offers of human comfort, jumped in the back seat of the funeral car, held the white casket, and yelled at me, "Come on! Let's get this over and done with!" The naked pain of trauma! The cremation was brief and stark.

Sadly for Vera and Jack and Annie and me, Jenny went back to Greg, to prostitution, and to alcohol and drugs. She was medicating her pain by inflicting more of it on herself. I would sometimes see her around Kings Cross and say, "Jenny, you know where I live. You know I am not there to shove Jesus down your throat. I just want to help in any way I can." Seemingly, it fell on deaf ears, until ten months later when she arrived on my doorstop late on a Sunday night. Greg had judged that she had not made enough money from prostitution that weekend, so he threw her into the wall of their dingy apartment. I took her, broken and bleeding, to St. Vincent's Hospital A&E department, and who should be there to receive us but Mary Maguire. Among other injuries, Greg had broken her arm, but that fracture led to the greatest break she could make. Jenny would not allow me to call the police, but she did let me call Vera and Jack. Hearing more bad news from me on the end of the phone, those wonderful parents jumped in their car at 10:00 p.m. and drove 536 miles (863km) through the night to Sydney.

The last time I saw Jenny was the next morning in the hospital car park as I helped her get into her parent's car for the ten-hour drive home. I stayed in touch with the three of them for a while until it was clear that I represented chapters in their family's life from which they wanted to move on.

In preparation for this chapter, I took the risk and contacted them again for the first time since 1993. I did not want to write this story without their permission. On her return to her parents' home, Jenny, who was then twenty-nine years of age, was appointed a thirty-two-year-old drug and alcohol counselor to her case. Daryl helped her get clean and sober and in the process saw beyond her very rough and tough exterior. He fell in love with her. As professional boundaries demand, he took a transfer to another city and had nothing to do with her for eighteen months. On transferring back, he met his now former client and twelve months later married her. They have two daughters and a son. The eldest is about to graduate from high school. Vera died four years ago, and Jack, a doting grandfather, lives with his loving family. Jenny works at an aged care facility. She has been clean and sober for more than twenty-one years. Nineteen years ago, the police rang and told Jenny that Greg had died from a shot-gun wound in the apartment they once shared. Her name was still on the lease. "I have to tell you, Father, I was relieved he was gone." Jenny and I were delighted to con-nect again over the phone, and she gave me permission to use the story you have just read. "It moved me to tears, Father, to realize how far I've come from those very dark days." It was clear, and rightly so, that any ongoing con-tact would unfairly complicate their lives. Sometimes, the most amazing of graces is to know when to let go.

For Jenny, her personal Good Friday did not have the last word in her life. How did the hope of Easter speak a word of faithful love in the face of utter and tragic pow-erlessness? It came through God's saving love in human form in extraordinary parents who kept coming back for more, and who seized the opportunity when it presented itself to rescue their child. They drove all night. It came in the love of a man who saw beyond the tough exterior and very complex story of his client. It transformed both of them. It has come through the love of four children, three of them living, which has drawn out of Jenny depths of goodness she never knew she had. It came through the Jesuits and a charge nurse at a hospital who were in the right places at the right times, doing what we could. It came through Annie, who did not stand outside Jenny's grief, but knew it from the inside, and so could give another grieving mother the greatest gifts of solidarity and hope. It is no wonder that from that day on I wanted Annie and Johnny and their family to become my friends too. And it came in the ministry of an alcoholic and homeless man who at 3:30 early one morning said, "I can't help you, but I can take you to people who can."

With the eyes of faith and a heart of love, the trauma of Good Friday can give way to trusting that some good, any good, can emerge from evil, and that life will prevail where death had been before. Ask Mary, the Mother of Jesus. She knows.

EASTER

Go to Galilee and Wait for Me There

*A*t the Easter Vigil, we enjoy listening to one of the most ancient and important hymns in the Church's tradition: the Exultet, which means "rejoice!" In the early Church, the deacon would have known the Exultet by heart. The honor of singing it was handed down from one generation to the next.

There are several images in the Exultet that help us name our joy: freedom from slavery; an end to fear; the triumph of life over death; and God's utter fidelity to his son, Jesus. The Exultet proclaims that God has not done this because we have earned or deserved it, but simply because he loves us. It is good to dwell on this last point for a moment. We have never done anything that can earn God's saving love. It is a completely unearned, unmerited, and undeserved gift, given to us in Jesus Christ. Our response to this gift is how we conduct our daily Christian lives, disclosing to others by our justice and joy that we have found the best way to announce that life can be found where others only see death.

The Easter Vigil is the holiest of nights because it seals the family covenant between God and us. We are coheirs with Jesus, sons and daughters of God. Is it any wonder, then, that heaven and earth are called to explode with joy?

As Christians, Easter joy is meant to mark our lives—though if some of us are truly joyful, we should start by telling our faces about it! Not that we can, or should, walk around perpetually smiling. Christian joy is more profound than that. It's about facing up to the most difficult and tragic moments in our lives, knowing that we don't have to be afraid, that God's faithful love will triumph in the end.

We all know this is easier said than done. Take, for example, one of the oldest Easter stories in the Gospels. The women are told twice to tell the disciples to go to Galilee where they will meet Jesus for themselves. The women do as they are asked, and the disciples make the trip. I've always wondered about Galilee. What a desolate journey that must have been for them. Believing the extraordinary story of Mary Magdalene and her companions, the disciples set out in fear of their lives, and in the hope of seeing Jesus raised from the dead. There were no reassurances from anyone's previous experience. No guidebooks or instructions about what to look for at the end. Not even a promise from Jesus, himself. Just an instruction, "Then go quickly and tell his disciples, 'He has been raised from the dead, and indeed he is going ahead of you to Galilee; there you will see him'" (Matt 28:7).

Galilee does not have to be a place for us. It's a situation, a frame of mind, or a choice we make. For example, of all the spiritual directors I have ever had in my life, one of the most insightful was going blind. A diocesan priest, Fr. Ray Crowley, had a genetic disease that was causing him to slowly and very surely lose his eyesight. While the doctors could stall the progress of the disease, he was told that there was nothing that could be done for him in the long term. What would any of us do if we knew we were eventually going to go blind?

After speaking to Ray about my own spiritual journey for several months, one day I plucked up the courage to ask him how he could be so calm in the face of his imminent and total visual impairment. He looked at me and said, "You know in the Gospels where the disciples are sent to Galilee to meet the Risen Lord? Well, I think I am being asked to go to blindness, and there I will meet the risen Lord in a totally different way." What faith! No wonder he was a spiritual director and I wasn't. His profound wisdom and insight stays with me to his day.

Our particular Galilee could be the desolate journey of physical, emotional, sexual or spiritual pain. It could be dashed promises, broken relationships, or unrealized hopes. Whatever it is, Easter night promises us that Christ is not only there when we arrive, he has gone ahead of us, to that desolate place, so that we might have loving arms in which to fall at journey's end.

The idea of the Easter journey being about new sight and insight is a rich one too. On Good Friday, when we always hear John's passion proclaimed, we hear three great questions:

- "Who are you looking for?"
- "What charge do you bring against this man?"
- "Aren't you another of that man's disciples?"

In John's Passion, the answers run,

- "Jesus of Nazareth"
- "King of the Jews"
- "I am not."

We come to the joy of the Easter Vigil because we seek Jesus of Nazareth, whose love has arrested us. We want to follow his way in our own discipleship, whatever path and complex destination upon which we may have to embark.

The fact that the third question of John's Passion is to Peter is interesting. Although Peter wanted to remain faithful to Jesus, fear got the better of him. Most of us can be empathetic to his plight. Faced with a choice between cutting and running and possible death, how many of us would choose death? And because actions always speak louder than words, every time we compromise the goodness of God within us, or work to undermine another person's rights to dignity and life, we join Peter around that fire denying that we are Christ's disciple. But the hapless, fickle, and impulsive Peter found his way to Galilee and that's where his discipleship began to come into its own. Some of us need a while for the Risen Christ's call to settle and mature, as well as some space to reflect upon the choices that have bought us to this moment. Then we can see what choices might see greater days ahead.

If we feel apprehensive, then this Easter allow Christ to arrest us with his peace. If we stand accused of destructive behavior, allow Christ to convert our hearts and change our lives. If we deny Christ by what we say or how we live, let's decide today to be as faithful to him as he is to us. Apprehension, accusation, and denial were not the last words in Jesus' life, and they are not meant to be so in our lives either.

In place of fear, the first Easter Vigil is a joyful call even to unknown places with unexpected results, and shows us that such fear can end in new life and fresh starts.

With the whole Church, we can make Mary Magdalene's invitation to the disciples our own. This Easter, let's go to Galilee, wherever and whatever it might be, and find the Lord there. Then, we can explode with joy and "Sing Christ Risen."

Tapers in the Fire

We're not exactly sure what happened during the first Easter. In the New Testament, we have seven accounts of an experience of the Risen Christ. There is the empty tomb tradition, the visual encounters with the Risen Christ, and later, in Acts 9, the equally powerful, auditory experience of St. Paul.

In fact, we are used to saying that Jesus "rose from the dead." The Scriptures, however, are much more careful with their language. They regularly tell us that Jesus was "raised" from the dead, that the resurrection is the action of the faithful, loving Father toward his Son. Who is doing what in the Easter story matters for us here and now.

So often, we may think that a life of faith is about us choosing God, and that even celebrating Easter is solely our own decision. The story of salvation that we hear every Easter Vigil is that faith is always God's initiative, to which we freely respond one way or another. One of the great things about the story of the first Easter is that God is not bound by our expectations. God is always greater than the Church. And even now, God is confounding the wise and revealing the kingdom to whomever God knows is receptive to hear it and live it out. In the Church, some of us struggle to believe that people outside its traditional structures can experience the loving and saving message of Christ Risen and be authentic apostles of the good news. In the midst of such doubters, it's good to remember that the women at Jesus' tomb were not believed by the men either. However, the women pressed on and simply witnessed to what they knew was true— that Christ's resurrection was revealed to them in a cemetery. They knew that God's life had found them, and that it was a matter of time until the others caught up to where God was, and what God was doing. When Easter continues to break in upon the world in our time, sometimes we need to get out of the way and let it go, and trust that God can be expected to do the unexpected.

Whatever the experience of the Risen Christ was like, the results were the same. Whoever encountered the Risen Lord went from believing that Jesus was dead to knowing he was alive. They were so convinced that Jesus was the Christ that many of them went on to give their lives as martyrs in bearing witness to it. They were prepared to face a hostile world because they knew that, in Christ, hope had the last word over suffering and death.

Life, courage, and hope! That's our Easter message,

and the world needs to hear it more than ever before. For some people, Easter can be seen as a great magical trick. Without us seeing how, Jesus escapes from the tomb, and the show goes on. But there are more than enough conjurers and tricksters around today, so the life, courage, and hope we celebrate at Easter is not about a sleight of hand, but about light coming out of darkness, and the promise that the love and fidelity of God had the last word in the life of Jesus, and can have the last word in our lives too.

The life, courage, and hope we celebrate every Easter Vigil is that God vindicated everything that Jesus was for us so that we might know God's utter solidarity with the human adventure, in the hope that we might be saved from the destruction of sin and death.

When we are betrayed by friends and abandoned by companions, denied by those closest to us, falsely accused, and had our integrity questioned, then the Risen Christ, who has been there first, will never deny or falsely accuse us, and will stand up with us and for us.

When we are judged and condemned, pushed from pillar to post and had our emotions laid bare, then the Risen Christ, who has been there first, offers us comfort and healing.

When we have felt the full weight of our burdens and the loneliness of dealing with them on our own, then the Risen Christ has been there first, and is our companion in the darkest of hours.

When we go through the heartbreak of having someone we love die, or the thousand other deaths that constitute our lives, then the Risen Christ has been there first to reassure us that there is no place he will not attend with us.

Christ is raised to new life so that every searching heart can find what will most satisfy; every human struggle is honored; and all our imaginations are blown away at just how God's love can act.

This is why the Easter Vigil is, above all, a ceremony of light, of Christ the Light raised from the dead, enlightening our lives, and enabling us to find our way. Even if this poetry might sound a little too lofty, the living of this goal is meant to be very practical.

Because God works in and through time, then how we spend our time in the service of our neighbor reveals how God works to save his people, drawing us into an ever-intimate embrace. Because of the first Easter day, we have become God's sons and daughters, coheirs of the kingdom.

Because God creates and works intelligently, in an ordered way so that we can discern his traces and follow them, we can move away from seeing life as seemingly random events, and begin to construct a meaningful life where every moment, most especially the ordinary and humdrum, can hold God's presence.

Because we believe in a patient God, who calls us to be likewise, then we can let go of "instant gratification" and look, long for, and wait for our patience to pay off.

And because we believe in Love itself, who took our flesh and bone, and was subjected to human violence as we are, we can find a path to peace and justice through nonviolence.

This is the context in which we can speak of being consumed by the light of Christ, and we can spend ourselves as fuel so that Christ's kingdom can come. Rather than simply flare and fade, we put the tips of our tapers into the holy fire of Easter and be so illuminated that our lives burn brightly in this world and the next.

Mary and Thomas

In the time after Easter, we hear about two of the most important saints in the Church: Mary Magdalene and Thomas. They both give us great hope but for very different reasons.

If we did a survey today of what words we associate with the name Mary Magdalene, chances are *prostitute* would come at the top of the list. The Christian tradition has not been very kind to Mary or her memory. She should sue for defamation! There is nothing in the New Testament about her being a woman in prostitution. Unfortunately, there are other women in the Gospels who have "a bad reputation in the town" or weep at Jesus' feet and wipe their tears away with their hair, or are caught in the "very act of adultery" or pour oil over Jesus' head. These women are not Mary of Magdala.

The first we hear of Mary Magdalene is that she has seven demons cast out of her by Jesus. We're not told what these demons are, but given what people wrongly thought at the time, they could have been a tummy complaint, acne, or a twitch! There is nothing in the text to suggest that they were sexual demons.

Andrew Lloyd Webber and Tim Rice, the playwrights and composer of *Jesus Christ Superstar* didn't do Mary Magdalene's saucy notoriety any favors by giving her character the song of the show: "I Don't Know How to Love Him." Curiously, some brides have wanted this song sung at their weddings over the years, to which I reply, "If you don't know how to love him, you shouldn't be here!" The rest of the song's chorus speaks of how many men she has had before and also in very many ways. I don't think that's what we want to say at a Nuptial Mass!

The most important thing we know about Mary Magdalene is that she is the first to experience the Risen Christ and is the first Christian missionary, the apostle to the apostles. One detail in John's Gospel is especially poignant. We are told that Mary encountered the Risen Christ while weeping outside Jesus' tomb. She felt a double loss on that first Easter Sunday. Not only was she grieving for the loss of the one whom she had seen tortured to death, but she also wept for what she thought was the ultimate insult inflicted on him—the desecration of his grave and the stealing of his corpse.

Mary Magdalene is the patron saint for those of us who have ever stood at tombs and wept. Furthermore, she shows us that, in the midst of any grief, Christ comes to us and calls us by name.

Because of Mary's tears and even more because of her evangelization, we believe that there is not a human being who has died who is not known to God by name. God makes no distinction between the rich and poor, whether we are from a developing or developed country, whether we are Christian, Muslim, or atheist; we are all called by name to share in his life according to the grace that has enabled us to do so. God knows not only our name; he knows our heart, our history, and our selves.

Jesus tells Mary Magdalene that there is no longer an exclusive God, but his God and Father is now Mary's God and Father. And maybe that's a good place to start. All people of faith and good will, whether they realize it or not, and some in vastly different cultural ways, seek and serve the same God.

The other thing that is repeatedly said about Mary Magdalene is that she is among the first "witnesses" to the resurrection. For us, the word *witness* usually means that we attest to the truth of events from personal experience and knowledge. The power of personal witness can hardly be exaggerated. And the same is true of Christian faith. To believe in Jesus Christ as Savior of the world might be attractive as a good idea or as an engaging concept, but the best witnesses have first-hand access to the truth. They don't believe in the idea of the resurrection; they have had a personal encounter with the Risen Christ themselves, and are bold enough to proclaim and live it.

This may be why in the early Church the word for witness and the word for martyr were one and the same. Anyone who was brave enough to publicly witness to the resurrection at that time potentially ended up giving his or her life for it. In fact, this is one of the two most compelling arguments for the reality of the resurrection. Within a generation after Jesus' death, people all over the Mediterranean world, most of whom had never seen Jesus, reported that they too had encountered the presence of the Risen Christ—that Jesus of Nazareth was not dead, but alive to them too. The other compelling reason that is difficult to counter is that these same people not only believed in the resurrection, but also were prepared to put their lives on the line for the person they had encountered.

And nothing has changed. This Easter we are called to be witnesses to Jesus, raised from the dead and alive to us here and now. This is no head trip, for in our own way, we are meant to put our bodies on the line for it. Like Mary Magdalene, our witness to life and forgiveness in Christ will have its costs in a world that is all too often given over to dealing in death, in all its forms, and addicted to revenge and retribution. So, too, we will have to pay a price for how we live and whom we challenge.

Maybe this is why we also have Thomas as a role model. The Gospel story about doubting Thomas has to be one of the most misunderstood episodes in the New Testament. If you're like me, for years we have been consoled by Thomas doubting that Jesus had been raised from the dead. We have been told that Thomas doubted Jesus. But let's read the story very carefully. It's not Jesus whom Thomas doubts, it's the disciples. In fact, when Jesus appears to them a week later, Thomas has the opportunity to share in the experience of the Risen Lord and, like the others, he immediately confesses Easter faith.

There are three elements in this story that should give us great comfort. The first is that Thomas does not doubt Jesus, but doubts the early Church, and not just in regard to a minor issue of discipline or procedure. He doubts the central Christian message: that God raised Jesus from the dead. Some of us, too, at various times in our lives, can have doubts about all sorts of things in our faith. There are very few Catholics who get through life without asking some serious questions of God, about Jesus, the Spirit, and the Church. These questions are good in themselves. They are necessary for a mature, adult faith. What we need to ensure is that we sincerely want answers to the questions we ask and not just use them to justify our wandering away from our faith. Thomas is the patron saint of all of us who sometimes struggle to believe what everyone else in the church seems to accept. And he is also the patron saint of those of us who seek the courage and patience to wait for the answers.

The second consoling fact to this story concerns the earliest Church. Even though they are filled with the presence of the Risen Lord, and although Thomas refuses to believe their witness, they remain faithful to him in his doubts. We know this because he is still with them a week later. They didn't expel him from the group or excommunicate him, they held on to him in the hope that he would experience the Lord for himself.

Sadly for us, today there are some who argue that Catholics who struggle with their faith should "shape up or ship out." While every group has its boundaries and there are limits from which people can dissent, we could take the earliest Church as our model and stay faithful to our doubters and help them come to see the transforming truth that has changed our lives.

The story of doubting Thomas was written for people like us who do not have access to the historical Jesus. The birth of the Church is an ongoing act of God's re-creation in every generation. It takes time, and people will be at different stages at different moments.

The third element of the story, even with its mystical details, counters a magical notion of what the resurrection is about. Jesus bears the marks of his torture and death. His glorified body, though different, is connected to how the disciples knew and loved him. They can recognize him through his words and his wounds. The earliest Christian community focused strongly on the wounds of the Risen Lord for two reasons: to affirm the fact that Christ, now raised from the dead, was the same person who had lived with them, and also to make sense of the physical wounds being inflicted on them for Christ's sake.

It seems, however, that words and wounds still make a claim on us today. We carry within us the death of the Lord—we all have our wounds. And we also know that, for many of us, it is precisely when we are wounded most deeply by life that our doubts in the presence of God can be greatest. The story of Thomas tells us that Christ takes our fears, doubts, and disbelief and transforms them into a powerful Christian witness, which can sustain us even in our struggle with life and faith. When we see this happening, when we see God taking into his hands the part of us we consider most unlovable and using it for good, then we want to cry out with the psalmist, "This is the LORD's doing; it is marvelous in our eyes" (Ps 118:23).

ASCENSION

Places at the Table

A teacher once told me of the time she asked her third graders to draw a picture of the ascension. Not unsurprisingly, most of them did a fairly conventional portrait of Jesus rising up onto the clouds. One of her students, David, who was a particularly gifted artist, had Jesus blasting off into the sky. Down the side of Jesus' pure white garment was the word NASA. As he showed his picture to the class, he provided all the sound effects that he imagined must have accompanied the first ascension. He concluded his presentation by saying without a hint of irony, "The Ascension must have been a real blast!" All the other kids said in chorus, "Awesome."

None of us can blame David for marrying our modern culture with an ancient story. In fact, if some of us are honest, David's "space shuttle Jesus" is not far from what we might also think.

The ascension stories, however, are not primarily interested in how or when Jesus got back to heaven. John and Paul never mention it at all. Mark and Matthew have it happening on the same day as the resurrection, and Luke has it occurring forty days after Easter on the same day as Pentecost. The one thing on which all the New Testament writers agree is where in heaven Jesus went and where he is presently—at God's right hand. This is brilliant theological shorthand: the right hand of God; the mountain top; and the forty days.

Even to this day, being on someone's right is a place of honor. Imagine being invited to the White House and finding that, of all the places you could have been placed, you are placed on the right hand of the president or the first lady?

In the Old Testament, being on the right hand of David, Samuel, or Elijah was to be the anointed and favored one, the true son or daughter. But it survives in popular culture too. *Game of Thrones* may be too explicit on every level for many people, but it remains the most-watched drama ever on subscription television. Of all the characters in this story, the most important person after the reigning monarch is the "Hand of the King." He is regularly just referred to as the *Hand* and wears a coveted pin to designate his authority to make decisions in the king's name.

In telling us, then, that Jesus is now at God's right hand, the Gospels use a formal phrase to announce that God affirms everything Jesus said and did on earth, and that he therefore is the One for us to follow. However, in the Gospels, Jesus goes one step further and teaches us that where he is, so shall we be, that he was going to prepare a place for us, and that in and through him we will have life and have it to the full.

The Feast of the Ascension is the day, each year,

where we remember and we celebrate that just as Jesus was welcomed to God's right hand, so, too, we may be welcomed to the symbolic right hand of Jesus. This is his promise, this is our faith, and this is the hope we're called to proclaim to the world.

And let's be clear about the invitation. There is nothing we have ever done, are doing, or will do that will get our name removed from the invitation list to the feast of Christ's kingdom. The challenge is accepting that we have a standing invitation and living lives worthy of the love that placed our name upon the list in the first place.

This parable demonstrates the point. In 1939, a father and son were famous art collectors. When World War II broke out, the son volunteered. In 1944, the son died in battle while rescuing another soldier. A year later, a young man came to see the father: "Sir, you don't know me, but I was with your son when he died. I want you to know he didn't suffer.

"I know you both loved art, and though this isn't much, I want you to have this painting." He gave the father a package. Inside was a portrait of the son. It was rough work, but the father welled up with tears. "It was the least I could do for your son because he saved my life on the battlefield. He died and I lived."

A few months later, the father died. At the art auction that followed, investors gathered from around the world. The first item up for bid was the portrait of the son.

The auctioneer tried to start the bidding, "$200... $100...Any bids? Any at all?" The investors called out, "Skip this one. Where are the Rembrandts?" Just then, a man spoke up from the back of the room. "I'll give you ten dollars for the painting. It's all the money I have." It was the gardener at the father's estate. He had known the father and the son for thirty years. The auctioneer brought down his gavel. "Sold for ten dollars!" An investor called back, "Can we get on with it now please?" But the auctioneer continued, "The auction is over. According to the will, whoever bought this painting would inherit the estate, including all the art."

No matter what they said, the wealthy investors couldn't buy their way into the inheritance. Only the one who had the eyes of love, and knew what he was looking at, inherited everything the Father and Son had to offer. That is what is promised in the ascension too.

The second image in the ascension is the mountain top. As we have seen in the transfiguration on Mount Tabor, almost every time someone in the Old Testament goes to the top of a mountain or up into the hill country, a significant encounter with God usually ensues. It is not by accident that one of God's titles in the Book of Exodus is *El Shaddai*, the god of the mountains. Mentioned over five hundred times in the Bible, mountains are where people felt close to God who was in heaven above: Abraham on Mount Moriah; Noah on Mount Ararat; Moses on Mount Sinai; Elijah on Mount Carmel; and David on Mount Zion. The importance of mountains continues in the New Testament as well: Jesus appoints the Twelve on a mountain; a famous Sermon is given on a Mount, and Jesus' temptations and the transfiguration occur on mountaintops. Even Mary, the carrier of the new covenant, rushes to the "hill country" to meet Elizabeth, the carrier of the last of the prophets.

What unite almost all these encounters on mountaintops are conversion, commissioning, and worship. That is the story of the ascension, too, where we encounter the Father, Son, and Holy Spirit in and through Christ's resurrection, and as a result, we are called to conversion of our life, to be commissioned to live Christ's life in our daily lives and to worship him in spirit and truth.

The third piece of shorthand in Luke's account of the ascension concerns the forty days. As we have already seen in regard to the season of Lent, the number forty indicates a time of formation. In the Bible, we have forty days of rain for Noah's flood, for Moses' fast, for Jonah inside the whale, and for the period between the resurrection and the ascension in Luke–Acts. The Israelites wander in the desert for forty years and Jesus enters the desert for forty days. Forty is the period of formation and preparation, and so, after a period of formation, Jesus sends out his disciples to proclaim the good news.

Having been formed by Christ's life, death, and resurrection, through this feast of ascension, we encounter and worship God in Christ on the mountaintop, where we are converted and commissioned to go out and proclaim that all people now possess the dignity of belonging to the family of God, because we have been invited to sit at Christ's right hand.

None of this is easy, but we have one eternal promise—as we go out, Christ abides before us, behind us, over and in us, within and without us, now and forever. Amen.

PENTECOST

The Gift of Ears

I admire our charismatic friends very much. They rightly love the Holy Spirit. I admire especially our Evangelical brothers and sisters because they have great faith and even greater courage. When I see them in any public space actively witnessing to the faith, I know I could not do what they do.

Mind you, I am not sure what it is about me, I must have the word *pagan* X-rayed into my forehead, but every time I go near a shopping mall and am minding my own business, I am accosted by our Evangelical friends. Almost invariably they come up to me and ask,

"Brother, have you given your life to Jesus Christ as your personal Lord and Savior?"

"Well, as a matter of fact I have."

"Has the Holy Spirit given you the gift of tongues?"

"I can, but I choose not to."

"Do you know the demands of living the life of the Lord?"

"Well, I hope poverty, chastity, and obedience for Christ for life is a decent push in the right direction."

Mind you, in mentioning poverty, I am reminded of my family, who, on seeing Jesuit real estate for the first time when I took my vows of poverty, chastity, and obedience said, "If this is poverty, I'd like to see how you guys live chastity—it all looks loose and fast to us."

The problem with Christian Evangelicals is that they often think the Holy Spirit can be reduced primarily to external signs. We know, however, from the first Pentecost and from our own experience that the Spirit works in both unpredictable and ordinary ways. The Holy Spirit, sent to live with us, continues to reveal God's truth to us, to advocate for us and, in turn, to glorify us in Christ. The Spirit seems to make a specialty of being present in the unexpected.

Pentecost faith challenges us to keep focusing on what exciting things the Spirit is doing in our own day. It's often a case of keeping up with her, and following her lead. For most of us, the traces of the Holy Spirit are only seen retrospectively.

However, if you're like me, you have been taught that the most public gift on display at the first Pentecost was that the apostles had the ability to speak in different tongues. But a more careful reading of the story reveals that the gift received that day was one equally of hearing, as much as it may have been of speaking. Luke recounts, "In our own languages we hear them speaking about God's deeds of power" (Acts 2:11). It wasn't so much the gift of tongues the earliest disciples received as much as their hearers received the gift of "ears," of listening.

In the Church today, when it comes to listening, some people mistake mono for stereo, uniformity for unity. At the first Pentecost, the earliest Christians had no such difficulty; they knew that speaking the same language was not as important as carefully listening to one another.

The early Church was a very complex and diverse community. Like today, they had great struggles to deal with—both inside and outside the community. Within a few years of the first Pentecost, there were fights between Peter and Paul over Jewish and Gentile converts. There were people who died for the faith and others who betrayed them to the authorities. Some Christians thought they were for Paul or Apollos rather than for Jesus, and still others thought the end of the world was nigh. The earliest Christian community was not a utopia.

Almost two thousand years later, in what Pope St. John XXIII hoped would be "a new Pentecost," Vatican II helped us to recover this most ancient tradition in our faith: that—in various, unexpected, and inculturated ways—the Holy Spirit has been present in all peoples, in every culture, and that whenever the gospel has been proclaimed in a new land, it already complements the best in that culture in that it seeks to affirm personal dignity, human worth, justice, care of the earth, and the promotion of forgiveness and peace.

Pentecost faith holds that while we build our faith on the believers who have gone before us, we have the responsibility to listen to our contemporary culture and put it into conversation with the gospel. That's why courage is one of the Holy Spirit's preeminent gifts. We are not allowed to retreat from the world but are sent out to enter into conversation with it, affirming what we can, and unashamedly standing against whatever demeans, oppresses, and is life denying. This is why we need to ask the Holy Spirit to hone our ears as well as prepare our tongues to clearly receive and proclaim the gospel of Christ in the market places of our own day and age. To speak to an increasingly secular world of the things of God requires prudence and wisdom, listening before speaking.

As chapter 2 of Acts continues, more traces of the Holy Spirit are in evidence. In fact, by the end of the account of the first Pentecost, we are given a list of the signs of the followers of Jesus: the wonders being worked through them; sharing their goods with one another and with the poor; praising God in the temple; breaking the bread at home; and welcoming into their community those who received their message of salvation.

If the first Pentecost was about hearing and speaking, it quickly became about being filled with wonder, sharing, praising God, breaking the bread, and receiving others with joy. If we really trust that the Holy Spirit abides with us still, then this impressive series of outcomes should be present among us here and now. While it can be daunting, St. Paul makes it practical: it is all about what we choose because that is what we become.

In his Letter to the Galatians, St. Paul says that the action of the Holy Spirit comes in the way that we are loving, joyful, peaceful, patient, kind, generous, faithful, gentle, and self-controlled. The problem with lists is they can be nice in themselves but too removed from providing a need to act upon them. However, the first Pentecost and the subsequent activity of the Holy Spirit tells us that the hallmarks of the presence of God is not in our words but in how we literally stand in the public square.

If we were charged for the crime of following the Holy Spirit in our daily choices, would there be enough evidence to convict us?

Pentecost is a wonderful, final Easter feast where we make and take Christ's Spirit as our own and listen before we speak; where we are open to wonder; where we share, especially with the poor; where we are filled with praise for how God works in and through the world; and discover Christ's unique presence in the "breaking of the bread," and are famous for our joyful hospitality.

If we all lived this out with courage, prudence, and wisdom, then the Holy Spirit would indeed re-create us, and renew the face of the earth.

Discerning the Traces

The word *Pentecost* comes from the Greek word *pentēkostē*, meaning "fiftieth." It's not by accident that this feast occurs on the fiftieth day after Easter Sunday and at the end of the seventh week. Numbers matter. Every invocation of seven is always an echo of the seven days of creation. In this case, it is a re-creation moment where frightened disciples are transformed into bold witnesses. In the Old Testament, fifty was the year of jubilee because it was rare for people to live beyond their fiftieth birthday. That's why three score and ten (seventy) is such a huge age in the Bible—very few people ever got there. Once in every lifetime, Israel marked a year of celebration.

This is where and why we have twenty-five-, fifty-, and one-hundred-year jubilees in our society to this day.

Of the many features of the Jubilee Year in Israel, three were consistent: they set slaves free, they canceled the debts, and they let the fields for crops go fallow. This meant that there was no such thing as life-time slavery among the Israelites, there was no cross-generational poverty, and they cared for the environment. It is no wonder the power of the Spirit is unleashed on the fiftieth day: we have been set free from the slavery of our sin by Christ, all our debts have been forgiven in Christ, and we are re-created as a new creation through Christ. This means we are meant to live as free sons and daughters of God: we forgive as we have been forgiven and we care for God's creation. What might that look like?

Our freedom might be noticeable by being more contemplative in our daily lives. Have you noticed the way many people answer the question, "How are you?" They say, "I'm tired, exhausted, finished, or spent." And that's the day they come back from vacation! Alternatively, they say, "I'm frantic, run off my feet, there's not enough hours in the day." We all seem to be frantic or exhausted. How do we know this is right? When was the last time you asked a friend how they were, and they replied, "I've got the life/work balance perfectly in order—thanks for asking"? We never hear that. I wonder what would happen if we replied, "Relaxed and laid back" or "Taking time to smell the roses." I don't think we would be believed, or we might get a lecture from our friends on how lucky we are not to be busy!

Sometimes, there's a competition about who can be

the most exhausted and the most frantic. I have a friend who always has to be the busiest person he knows. If I ever say I have been busy lately, he will reply, "You're busy? I'm run off my feet!" And I want to say, "John, I'm sorry, I should've realized we're playing the 'I'm the busiest person in the room competition' and I know you *always* have to win that one."

As Christians, we have to be careful about this busyness competition. Being active in our lives and engaged with the world around us is a gift, but if we are honest about our busyness, some of it is not virtuous. It's about denial, avoidance, or trying to stay up with our peer group. In John's account of the first Pentecost, the primary gift Jesus' Spirit bestows on the disciples is peace. It's curious that, just as we all compete with each other to be the busiest person we know, we also complain that what we really want is "some peace and quiet." We can't have it both ways. Compulsive frantic activity is the enemy of peace.

Sometimes we can think that peace and quiet is sitting in the lotus position in a darkened room. It can be, but Christ's gift of peace is more robust. Peace is like all the best things in life: an attitude of mind and a habit born of consistently making good choices. Some people can do a large amount of work and be quite serene about it. Peace, for them, is a way of life, of being a contemplative in action.

It is worth noting that before Jesus, Seneca the Younger (4 BC–65 AD) noticed how most of his friends and acquaintances were lacking peace. He wrote a famous book on anger and how to deal with it. He especially noticed that his richest friends were the angriest of all. Seneca came to believe that the reason so many people were agitated was that they had an unreasonable expectation about how smoothly their day would go. Those who were rich thought their money would buy them an easier life in every way and so when it didn't, they became the angriest of all.

If Seneca is right and we want more peace and quiet, we have to have realistic expectations of each day and factor in the things that might go wrong.

The second movement is forgiveness. Don't tell some Christians this, but Jesus had very little to say about sexual sins in the Gospels. That does not mean they are unimportant; it is just a fact that Jesus has only a few things to say about sexuality. The two biggest sins in the Gospels—the ones that Jesus comes back to again and again—are first, hypocrisy, and second, a lack of forgiveness. There is hardly a page of the Gospels where Jesus does not condemn those who say one thing and do another, and those who cannot or will not forgive.

No one, least of all Jesus, is pretending that forgiveness is easy. In the fifth century, St. Augustine said that forgiveness was like a mother who had two lovely daughters called justice and compassion. When we are reconciled with our enemies, we do not pretend harsh words and actions were not done and said. We hold others to account for what they have done and failed to do, but we do so compassionately, imaging what the world might be like from their point of view. Sometimes we have to start by forgiving ourselves. Wherever we start, and however we begin, forgiveness is an inescapable element in following Jesus.

Again, Seneca argued that the more aware we are of the frailties in ourselves, in others and life, the more peace we would have. He also noted that this, in turn, would lead to fewer occasions when we would need to ask or give forgiveness in the first place. In John's Gospel, after peace, the next great Pentecost gift Jesus bequeaths his disciples is forgiveness, and this is contingent on us doing for others what God has done for us—offering mercy and forgiveness.

Finally holding creation in right relationship has two elements: the first is the externally created order, and the second is the one we create for ourselves.

Since Pope Francis's lyrical encyclical, *Laudato Si'*, it is impossible now not to know of our moral obligations to care for creation, to treat it as the gift it is. We are called to be stewards, not wreckers of God's good gifts:

> If the simple fact of being human moves people to care for the environment of which they are a part, Christians in their turn realize that their responsibility within creation, and their duty towards nature and the Creator, are an essential part of their faith. (#64)

> Our insistence that each human being is an image of God should not make us overlook the fact that each creature has its own purpose. None is superfluous. The entire material universe speaks of God's love, his boundless affection for us. Soil, water, mountains: everything is, as it were, a caress of God. (#84)

> A healthy relationship with creation is one dimension of overall personal conversion,

which entails the recognition of our errors, sins, faults and failures, and leads to heartfelt repentance and desire to change. (#218)

The universe unfolds in God, who fills it completely. Hence, there is a mystical meaning to be found in a leaf, in a mountain trail, in a dewdrop, in a poor person's face. The ideal is not only to pass from the exterior to the interior to discover the action of God in the soul, but also to discover God in all things. (#233)[12]

Rather than see Pope Francis's words in any idiosyncratic or exotic way, we can see that our care for the earth is one of the first fruits of Pentecost.

Continuous with our right and harmonious relationship with the earth is the right ordering of our own lives. The church's venerable tradition regarding discernment—to finding the action of the Holy Spirit—testifies to the wider social impact of our personal decisions.

St. Ignatius Loyola left the church a guide for working out how we can tell if and where the Holy Spirit is leading us. My summary of them is the following:

1. Trust the commonplace, the ordinary, the everyday. Live in the here and now. Sometimes we live in an unhealed past or an unknown future, whereas God may be found right under our nose, here and now. "The good can be the enemy of the better." We are both attacked at the most vulnerable parts of ourselves, and allured by the

narcotics of modern living (drugs, alcohol, sex, work, gambling, technology, and shopping), which never take away the pain of living but temporarily mask its effects.

2. Do not make a decision when we are down; allow the crisis to pass. Sometimes we make the worst decisions when we are under pressure. It is always better to let a crisis pass and then, in calmer surroundings, weigh up all our options.

3. Be suspicious of "the urgent." Sometimes we have to make a big decision quickly. Buying some time, any time, is always helpful for working out the best course of action. The good spirit brings a sense of perspective and priority to problems.

4. Be humble enough to take wise advice. We are not meant to be "rocks and islands," operating on our own. We need the wisdom of our families and most trusted friends, the Church, and sometimes professionals to inform our consciences and make the best possible decisions before God.

5. There are always patterns to the action of the good and bad spirit in our lives. Sometimes we think something "came out of nowhere." Sometimes it does, but most times the good and bad that beset us have a history and a context. We have to train ourselves to read the signs of both, cultivate the things that are good and see the empty promises of the bad spirit and how it lead us into dead ends. A daily examination of conscience helps us to see the pattern of the Holy Spirit.

6. A good or better decision is just one decision away. The bad spirit always convinces us we are trapped and there is no way out, diminishing our memory so we keep repeating destructive behavior even though it never helps, it alienates us, and does not help us deal with our situation.

7. The good spirit connects us and frees us to bring out into the open anything we keep buried in the dark. The bad spirit divides, isolates, and locks us in our fears. Every time we are transparent with those we love and trust, the good spirit is at work. There is nothing we have ever done, are doing, or will do, that will stop God from loving us. There is nothing that God cannot forgive and heal, but we have to start with owning up to who we are and what we have done. Then, anything and everything is possible.

8. The Holy Spirit is always present where a community of faith in God gathers. In the community, we discover that we are not the only ones who have ever had to make a particular choice or that we are not the first to face similar problems.

9. No work for the coming of the kingdom is too small, irrelevant, or inconsequential. We can often be conned into thinking that our relatively small and daily acts of kindness do not count for much in the spiritual scheme of things. Wrong. If there were more evil actions than loving actions in our world on any one day, the earth would be personally unlivable. Simple and selfless acts of kindness might go unreported, but they change

the world by enabling Christ's love to break through into the world of our daily lives.

10. Fidelity is one of the greatest gifts of the Spirit. Even in the face of opposition and other choices, remaining faithful is a heroic act of love. That said, the Gospel calls us to "die unto self," not to "kill self." It is never God's will, for example, for a person to stay in a physically, emotionally, and spiritually violent relationship. Ignatius encourages us to imagine we are advising our best friend about the matter we have under discernment. What would your counsel be? Alternatively, imagine being on our death bed. What choices do we wish we had made as we reviewed our life. Hopefully, it would be the most loving, faithful, and hopeful one.

Pentecost is God's promise to abide with us come what may. Living in the power and love of the Spirit is an intensely practical affair. The forty days of Lenten formation is meant to see us flourish into the fifty days of Easter as we claim afresh our freedom, our forgiveness, and our re-creation in Christ.

This is why we hope and pray that each year these seasons only get better and richer as they "Easter in us."

CORPUS CHRISTI

Broken and Shared, Poured Out and Sent

On October, 13, 1972, a chartered flight carrying forty-five people, including a rugby union team and their entourage from Montevideo, Uruguay, crashed in the Andes on its way to Santiago, Chile. More than a quarter of the passengers died on impact, while several others quickly succumbed to cold and injury. Of the twenty-seven who were alive a few days after the accident, another eight were killed by an avalanche that swept over their shelter in the wreckage. The final sixteen survivors were rescued on December 23, 1972, more than two months after the crash. We now know that all of these survivors resorted to cannibalism to survive. This case started an extraordinary ethical debate about whether it is ever ethical to eat another human being.

Whatever the extreme and specific ethical arguments for cannibalism might be, the thought of eating another person is repulsive to most of us. However, since the second century, some people outside the church often think that Christians are cannibals, feasting on Jesus' flesh and blood. The feast of the body and blood of Christ does not turn us into cannibals; we are not eating Jesus' liver, brain, and bones. It is meant to make us radicals—radically embodying the pattern of Christ's life, death, and resurrection in our own lives.

The best traditions in the Church have always been very careful in the language they use about how Jesus is present in the Eucharist. In the *Catechism*, when it speaks of the eucharistic real presence, it never refers to "Jesus" but always to "Christ." This distinction matters. The Eucharist is a sacrament of Easter.

Popular piety and legends that speak too explicitly about the physicality of the Eucharist have not helped. As a Catholic, I believe that Christ, raised by God from the dead, is fully and truly present to me in the consecrated bread and wine at Mass. In 1 Corinthians 15, St. Paul was at pains to rebut two extreme views about the glorified body of Christ: a crude physicalism, where the glorified body of Christ was simply a resuscitation of his corpse; and an overspiritualization where the Christ raised from the dead was an ethereal ghost.

The *Catechism* puts the issue succinctly:

> The glorious body (is) not limited by space and time but able to be present how and when he wills; for Christ's humanity can no longer be confined to earth. (*CCC* 645)

The risen body and blood of Christ is found in the experience of Easter it signifies, an encounter that transcends the boundaries of human weakness, but at the same time raises it up and heals all the wounds of the body. The divine presence of Christ lives in and through the redeemed physical world, but is not bound or contained by it.

For the first few centuries, Christians adored Christ as they consumed communion. Saints and bishops in the early Church encouraged this, but it was always linked to the actual celebration of the Eucharist. Reservation of the Blessed Sacrament was rare, and then mainly for the sick. From the fifth century onward, a major change occurred as people increasingly believed (because theologians told them so) that they were not worthy to receive the Eucharist, so, for many, their adoration of the Risen Lord took the place of communing with him.

By the high medieval period, we have descriptions about people rushing from church to church upon hearing the bells of the elevation so they could gaze upon the Blessed Sacrament. If the priest was short and the host could not be seen by the congregation at the back of the church they were known to chant "higher, higher, higher." By the eleventh century, a large number of Catholics simply never received communion, and so only felt close to Christ through the act of adoration. This was so much so that in 1215, the church had to enact a law requiring Catholics to receive communion at least once a year, at Eastertime. That law is with us to this day.

Associated with this lack of worthiness was an association that adoring the Blessed Sacrament was akin to being invited to enter into the heavenly court to look upon Christ the king. Hence, and in living memory, Benediction of the Blessed Sacrament almost always involved bejeweled copes and monstrances, flickering candles and elaborately adorned altars. We were welcomed into the regal presence.

Many of us have warm memories of these richly theatrical liturgies, the Divine Praises, and the Latin hymns. It all worked to create a magical atmosphere because gazing upon the host was thought to impart an intense power and deep consolation.

At the Second Vatican Council, the church went "back to the sources" of its own tradition, and we discovered that while the act of adoration is important and consistent with the intensity of our love—in a similar way to how we say two people who are totally in love with one another "adore each another"—receiving the Risen Lord in holy communion was the more ancient part of our tradition and a more complete act. Indeed, Vatican II also reminded us that while we Catholics believe that Christ is uniquely and intimately present in the bread of life and the cup of salvation, we also believe that Christ's real presence comes to us in the word of God, in the gathered assembly of God's people, and in the person of the ministers.

We came to see that, while we can never be worthy of God's unconditional and freely given love, presence, and goodness, it is given to us so that we might live lives worthy of it. Christ's saving love and invitation enables us to be invited, healed, forgiven, and welcomed. Christ never intended the bread of life only for the saints, a feast for the privileged few. It's not a private devotion. It's meant to be something that empowers "loved sinners" to go out and transform the world for Christ's sake.

Sometimes a few believers can speak of the Eucharist as a magical act. Jesus counters such a notion by telling us that he gives us himself "for the life of the world." There is an important difference between grace and magic.

One is a trick for a show. The other is the power of love, which expresses itself in faith, hope, and service. The Eucharist is not intimate and unique because it is magic. It's not intimate and unique because we only gaze upon the elements. The Eucharist is intimate and unique because ordinary earthly signs of bread and wine are transformed by God's love and are consumed in faith. As we eat and drink these elements, Christ becomes part of us, and we come alive in Christ.

In the fifth century, St. Augustine taught his people that if they truly loved the Eucharist they would become what they eat. The same is true for us today. By receiving into our hands the bread and wine of Easter at Christ's feast—blessed and broken, poured out and shared—we say, "Amen" (literally: "So be it") to becoming the same in Christ, blessed, broken, poured out, and shared in love. We commune with God and God with us in the Eucharist so that, just as our earthly gifts are transformed into Christ, we might become Christ in the world. As noted earlier, the most common Catholic word for the Eucharist, *Mass*, means "to be sent." Christ sustains with this sacred meal for the mission upon which he sends us.

Again, St. Augustine, in a sermon on the Eucharist on August, 9, 413, wrote that the Eucharist was about three things: goodness, unity, and charity. Augustine taught that if we were not better people, working for unity and loving each other away from the Eucharist, then it has failed to achieve its purpose. Augustine knew that whenever and wherever our lives are broken and poured out in love, we will discover that Corpus Christi is not just about falling down in adoration before the Blessed Sacrament, but also being sent by Christ to serve our sisters and brothers as generously as we can with sacrificial love, especially the poorest of the poor.

Understood in these ways, the body and blood of Christ moves away from celebrating only the static presence of God in the Blessed Sacrament, to the dynamic living out of this feast in our daily lives; in doing so, we discover that Corpus Christi is the most moveable and radical of feasts.

THE MOST HOLY TRINITY

Firmly I Believe and Truly

The first time I preached on the feast of the Most Holy Trinity was during my appointment as a deacon at St. Canice's, Kings Cross. As noted earlier, Kings Cross is the red-light district of Sydney, and so the congregations there are a wonderful mixture of all God's children, and some of them very colorful indeed.

I was the luckiest deacon in Australia because my seventy-year-old Irish Jesuit parish priest, Fr. Donal Taylor, never directly said no to any of my new and trendy ideas. He would simply say, "I'd be slow on that one." One Friday before Trinity Sunday, I told Donal that I was going to preach that while Father, Son, and Holy Spirit were privileged names for God, they did not exhaust the possibilities, and that God could helpfully be styled as our mother. Doubling over in the chair he said, "I'd be slow on that one," which I was to discover later was his way of saying, "No, don't do it!"

At the Vigil Mass, we had our usual parishioners, 120 young women who were boarders at St. Vincent's

Catholic High School, and in the front pew was Con, the most famous homeless person in Kings Cross. During my advocacy for the maternity of God, Con jumped up and voiced what was probably a majority position in the church: "God's not our mother! Mary's our mother, and God's our father." Turning to Fr. Donal, he said, "Father Donal, this idiot hasn't got a clue." He then turned to the congregation and shouted, "And if you are listening to this BS, you need your head read!" and marched out of the church. The congregation erupted with laughter and 120 young women thought this was the best Mass they'd ever been to. So I looked at Donal, and then at the congregation and said what could only be said in such a situation— "In the Name of the Father and of the Son and of the Holy Spirit. Amen"—and sat down. As I did, Donal turned to his unteachable deacon and mocked me, saying, "I told you to be slow on that one."

Later, over dinner, Fr. Donal asked me, "Are you going to give the same homily tomorrow?" "I am not sure if you noticed," I replied, "but it did not go down a treat tonight." "Oh, you leave Con to me. He swore during Mass, and I won't have it, so I will warn him off the place for a week. But I want you to give the same homily." "Really? I thought it was not your cup of tea," I replied. "Look, I am still coming to grips with God our Father, let alone thinking about God our Mother, but there are those of us who need to know that father is not the only name for God, and that just because we name God does not mean we can control God."

The mystery of the Trinity means that, in whatever way we portray God as Father, Son, and Spirit, it will always be inadequate and incomplete. None of us have ever seen God or the Holy Spirit. No one has a portrait of Jesus. All the images and words we use for the Trinity are more a reflection of our faith than the final word about God. God is always more than any name we use or any concept we have. The special insight we celebrate in this feast is that relationships are at the very center of who God is.

It took the early Christians four hundred years to grasp fully what Jesus was on about when he spoke of his relationship to the Father and the Spirit. They struggled to understand how and why God would have three faces and yet exist as One Being—loving as One, acting as One. They settled the "how" of the Trinity's nature by teaching us that the persons of the Trinity are coequal, cosubstantial, and coeternal. The persons within the Trinity empower each other, and are equally present in every act of God in the world, be it creating, redeeming, or making holy. One person of the Trinity was not created by another person. They just are, and always have been.

The early Christians settled the "why" of the Trinity by reflecting on the fact that their experience of the Father, Son, and Holy Spirit was an encounter of love. They knew the core of God was not an idea or a principle, but was a loving relationship.

Furthermore, the early Christians knew that they were invited into this relationship. A famous icon of the Trinity depicts them at a table where there are four place settings. The final place, in the lower half of the painting, invites the viewer to take the seat and join them. This is what gives us our greatest dignity and urges us to share this message with everyone we meet.

What was true for them is true for us. Consider this: we believe that the God who creates, redeems, and sustains the world seeks us out and invites us into a loving relationship. What a privilege! What an invitation! What a God!

It also follows that if relationships are at the core of God, then, for those who accept the invitation into the Trinity's embrace, relationships are meant to be our core business too. We are not meant to be isolated believers or private disciples. The degree to which we understand today's feast will be shown in the care we take in our many and varied relationships, be they social, intimate, professional, civic, or international.

Some people argue that the mystery of the Trinity is too much to deal with logically. Of course, the problem is that the Trinity is not a problem for our minds to solve, but a relationship to be drawn into and to savor. In the power of the Spirit, through the gift of the Father, and in the saving love of the Son, we have found our way home— an eternal home of equality and substance. Not that we are coeternal, cosubstantial, or coequal with the Trinity, but through our baptisms we have been empowered by them to share in their inner and divine life, which, because they choose it this way, cannot help but overflow in goodness and creativity toward us.

Imagination, it seems, is the key to believing in the Trinity.

There are many things in the world I can't explain— scientific discoveries, genetic dispositions, why one human being would love another, how some people can forgive, or how good some of us are to others while asking for nothing in return. While I can't explain these things, I can imagine them because I have witnessed them.

Indeed, I can imagine a world where we speak the truth to each other gently and respectfully.

I can imagine a world where we share from our abundance with those who have nothing.

I can imagine a world where understanding takes the place of retribution.

And if I can imagine what others think is unimaginable about our world, I can also imagine an empowering God—Father, Son, and Holy Spirit.

Many people have tried to give us helpful images regarding the Trinity. St. John of Damascus said the Trinity was like a dance, a *Pas de trois*. St. Ignatius Loyola described it as three notes in a single chord. St. Patrick famously used the three-leaf clover as a teaching aid to get the point across to the Irish, and St. Augustine thought the Trinity acted in unison in the same way that memory, intelligence, and will does within each of us.

All these images are helpful, but when I witness the life of the Trinity in action, the leap of faith is even easier. When I see Christians treating others as equals, especially those they don't like, and according them rights and dignity as children of God, then I can move beyond imagining the life of the Trinity to experiencing it firsthand.

It's not by accident that in our Catholic tradition the usual moment we invoke the Trinity is when we make the sign of the cross. There is a cost for living out this relationship in our daily lives. Every time we profess the

Trinity, we recommit ourselves to die to self so that God's saving love may be realized for everyone, everywhere, and that, empowered to be beacons of equality and exemplars of what's best in redeemed human nature, this feast keeps our feet on the ground and an eye on eternity.

NOTES

1. Tom Conry, "Ashes," (1978 New Dawn Music); lyrics available in *Glory and Praise*, OCP Publications, 1997.

2. Pope Francis, *Laudato Si'*, see http://w2.vatican.va/content/francesco/en/encyclicals/documents/papa-francesco_20150524_enciclica-laudato-si.html.

3. Hugh Mackay, *The Good Life: What Makes a Life Worth Living?* (Melbourne: Pan Macmillan Australia, 2013), 12ff.

4. See "Pope Francis: The Church Is a House of Joy," December 15, 2013, http://www.news.va/en/news/pope-francis-the-church-is-a-house-of-joy.

5. Pope Francis, homily during Mass on Friday, May 10, 2013, in the Casa Santa Marta chapel. See http://www.catholicnewsagency.com/news/pope-sad-christian-faces-are-like-pickled-peppers/.

6. Johannes Baptist Metz, *Poverty of Spirit* (New York: Paulist Press, 1968, 1998), 14.

7. Ibid., 17.

8. Thomas Merton, *Love and Living* (New York: Farrar, Straus and Giroux, 1979), 112.

9. Hymn to Christ the King, "Hail Redeemer, King Divine," refrain; music: Grattan Flood 1859–1928; text: Fr. Patrick Brennan, CSSR.

10. Augustine, sermon 272 (On the Day of Pentecost—To the Catechumens, Concerning the Sacrament).

11. Didier Rimaud, "In Remembrance of You," translated and set to music by Christopher Willcock, SJ (Oregon: OCP Publications, 1988).

12. Pope Francis, *Laudato Si'*.